THEOLOGY OF CULTURE

TO HANNA and GERHARD COLM

Paul Tillich

THEOLOGY

OF CULTURE

EDITED BY ROBERT C. KIMBALL

OXFORD UNIVERSITY PRESS
London   Oxford   New York

OXFORD UNIVERSITY PRESS

Oxford   London   Glasgow

New York   Toronto   Melbourne   Wellington

Kuala Lumpur   Singapore   Jakarta   Hong Kong   Tokyo

Nairobi   Dar es Salaam   Cape Town

Delhi   Bombay   Calcutta   Madras   Karachi

ISBN: 978-0-19-500711-4

© 1959 by Oxford University Press, Inc.

Library of Congress Catalogue Card Number: 59-9814

First published by Oxford University Press, New York, 1959

First issued as an Oxford University Press paperback, 1964

Foreword

The purpose of this book is indicated in its title: *Theology of Culture*. The title is an abbreviation of the title of my first published speech, given in the Berlin section of the *Kant-Gesellschaft*: *Über die Idee einer Theologie der Kultur* (On the Idea of a Theology of Culture). It is a source of great satisfaction to me that after the passing of forty years I can take the title for this volume from my first important public speech.

In spite of the fact that during most of my adult life I have been a teacher of Systematic Theology, the problem of religion and culture has always been in the center of my interest. Most of my writings—including the two volumes of *Systematic Theology*—try to define the way in which Christianity is related to secular culture. Using some of these writings, the present volume attempts to show the religious dimension in many special spheres of man's cultural activity. This dimension, which is described in the first section of the book, is never absent in cultural creations even if they show no relation to religion in the narrower sense of the word. This dimension, and not any ecclesiastical control of cultural creativity, was, and is, meant when the phrase "Theology of Culture" is used.

My thanks are extended to my assistant Mr. Robert Kimball, who chose and edited from amongst a large number of printed and unprinted articles and papers those which appeared most fitting for this volume. My thanks are also extended to the Oxford University Press, especially Miss Marion Hausner, and to Grace Cali Leonard and Lorna Thomas Kimball, who assisted in the preparation of the manuscript.

PAUL TILLICH

Cambridge, Massachusetts
February 1959

Acknowledgments

Acknowledgments are due the publishers who have granted permission for the use of essays which have previously appeared in print. The majority of these essays have been altered for the present volume. Following are the references for each chapter:

I, *Man's Right to Knowledge*, 2nd Ser., Columbia University Press, 1954.

II, *Union Seminary Quarterly Review*, I, 4, May, 1946.

III, Unpublished.

IV, *World Christian Education*, 2nd quarter, 1956.

V, *The Christian Scholar*, xxxviii, 3, Sept., 1955.

VI, *The Christian Scholar*, xl, 4, Dec., 1957.

VII, *Journal of the History of Ideas*, v, 1, Jan., 1944.

VIII, *Faith and Freedom*, ix, 25 (part 1), Autumn, 1955.

IX, *The Union Review*, II, 1, November, 1940.

X, *Ministry and Medicine in Human Relations*, Iago Galdston, editor; International Universities Press, Inc., New York, 1955.

XI, *The Church School in Our Time*, St. Paul's School Centennial Publication, Concord, N.H., 1957.

XII, *The Cultural Migration*, W. Rex Crawford, editor; University of Pennsylvania Press, 1953.

XIII, *The Contemporary Scene*, The Metropolitan Museum of Art, New York, 1954.

XIV, *Commentary*, v, 6, June, 1948.

XV, *Union Seminary Quarterly Review*, vii, 4, June, 1952.

R. C. K.

Contents

THEOLOGY OF CULTURE

I. BASIC CONSIDERATIONS

I

Religion as a Dimension
in Man's Spiritual Life

As soon as one says anything about religion, one is questioned from two sides. Some Christian theologians will ask whether religion is here considered as a creative element of the human spirit rather than as a gift of divine revelation. If one replies that religion is an aspect of man's spiritual life, they will turn away. Then some secular scientists will ask whether religion is to be considered a lasting quality of the human spirit instead of an effect of changing psychological and sociological conditions. And if one answers that religion is a necessary aspect of man's spiritual life, they turn away like the theologians, but in an opposite direction.

This situation shows an almost schizophrenic split in our collective consciousness, a split which threatens our spiritual freedom by driving the contemporary mind into irrational and compulsive affirmations or negations of religion. And there is as much compulsive reaction to religion on the scientific side as there is on the religious side.

Those theologians who deny that religion is an element of man's spiritual life have a real point. According to them, the meaning of religion is that man received something which does not come *from* him, but which is given *to* him and may stand against him. They insist that the relation to God is not a human possibility and that God must first relate Himself to man. One could summarize the intention of these theologians in the sentence that religion is not a creation of the human spirit (spirit with a small s) but a gift of the divine Spirit (Spirit with a capital S). Man's spirit, they would continue, is creative with respect to itself and its world, but not with respect to God. With respect to God, man is receptive and only receptive. He has no freedom to relate himself to God. This, they would add, is the meaning of the classical doctrine of the Bondage of the Will as developed by Paul, Augustine, Thomas, Luther, and Calvin. In the face of these witnesses, we certainly ask: Is it then justified to speak of religion as an aspect of the human spirit?

The opposite criticism also has its valid point. It comes from the side of the sciences of man: psychology, sociology, anthropology, and history. They emphasize the infinite diversity of religious ideas and practices, the mythological character of all religious concepts, the existence of many forms of non-religion in individuals and groups. Religion, they say (with the philosopher Comte), is characteristic for a special stage of human development (the mythological stage), but it has no place in the scientific stage in which we are living. Religion, according to this attitude, is a transitory creation of the human spirit but certainly not an essential quality of it.

If we analyze carefully these two groups of arguments, we discover the surprising fact that although they come from opposite directions, they have something definite in common. Both the theological and the scientific critics of the belief that religion is an aspect of the human spirit define religion as man's relation to divine beings, whose existence the theological critics assert and the scientific critics deny. But it is just this idea of religion which makes any understanding of religion impossible. If you start with the question whether God does or does not exist, you can never reach Him; and if you assert that He does exist, you can reach Him even less than if you assert that He does not exist. A God about whose existence or non-existence you can argue is a thing beside others within the universe of existing things. And the question is quite justified whether such a thing does exist, and the answer is equally justified that it does not exist. It is regrettable that scientists believe that they have refuted religion when they rightly have shown that there is no evidence whatsoever for the assumption that such a being exists. Actually, they have not only not refuted religion, but they have done it a considerable service. They have forced it to reconsider and to restate the meaning of the tremendous word *God*. Unfortunately, many theologians make the same mistake. They begin their message with the assertion that there is a highest being called God, whose authoritative revelations they have received. They are more dangerous for religion than the so-called atheistic scientists. They take the first step on the road which inescapably leads to what is called atheism. Theologians who make of God a highest being who has given some people information about Himself, provoke inescapably the resistance of those who are told they must subject themselves to the authority of this information.

Against both groups of critics we affirm the validity of our subject: religion as an aspect of the human spirit. But, in doing so, we take into consideration the criticisms from both sides and the elements of truth in each of them.

When we say that religion is an aspect of the human spirit, we are saying that if we look at the human spirit from a special point of view, it presents itself to us as religious. What is this view? It is the point of view from which we can look into the depth of man's spiritual life. Religion is not a special function of man's spiritual life, but it is the dimension of depth in all of its functions. The assertion has far-reaching consequences for the interpretation of religion, and it needs comment on each of the terms used in it.

Religion is not a special function of the human spirit! History tells us the story of how religion goes from one spiritual function to the other to find a home, and is either rejected or swallowed by them. Religion comes to the moral function and knocks at its door, certain that it will be received. Is not the ethical the nearest relative of the religious? How could it be rejected? Indeed, it is not rejected; it is taken in. But it is taken in as a "poor relation" and asked to earn its place in the moral realm by serving morality. It is admitted as long as it helps to create good citizens, good husbands and children, good employees, officials, and soldiers. But the moment in which religion makes claims of its own, it is either silenced or thrown out as superfluous or dangerous for morals.

So religion must look around for another function of man's spiritual life, and it is attracted by the cognitive function. Religion as a special way of knowledge, as mythological imagination or as mystical intuition—this seems to give a home to religion. Again religion is admitted, but as subordinate to pure knowledge, and only for a brief time. Pure knowledge, strengthened by the tremendous success of its scientific work, soon recants its half-hearted acceptance of religion and declares that religion has nothing whatsoever to do with knowledge.

Once more religion is without a home within man's spiritual life. It looks around for another spiritual function to join. And it finds one, namely, the aesthetic function. Why not try to find a place within the artistic creativity of man? religion asks itself, through the mouths of the philosophers of religion. And the artistic realm answers, through the mouths of many artists, past and present, with an enthusiastic affirmative, and invites religion not only to join with it but also to acknowledge that art *is* religion. But now religion hesitates. Does not art express reality, while religion transforms reality? Is there not an element of unreality even in the greatest work of art? Religion remembers that it has old relations to the moral and the cognitive realms, to the good and to the true, and it resists the temptation to dissolve itself into art.

But now where shall religion turn? The whole field of man's spiritual life is taken, and no section of it is ready to give religion an adequate place. So religion turns to something that accompanies every activity of man and every function of man's spiritual life. We call it feeling. Religion is a feeling: this seems to be the end of the wanderings of religion, and this end is strongly acclaimed by all those who want to have the realms of knowledge and morals free from any religious interference. Religion, if banished to the realm of mere feeling, has ceased to be dangerous for any rational and practical human enterprise. But, we must add, it also has lost its seriousness, its truth, and its ultimate meaning. In the atmosphere of mere subjectivity of feeling without a definite object of emotion, without an ultimate content, religion dies. This also is not the answer to the question of religion as an aspect of the human spirit.

In this situation, without a home, without a place in which to dwell, religion suddenly realizes that it does not need such a place, that it does not need to seek for a home. It is at home everywhere, namely, in the depth of all functions of man's spiritual life. Religion is the dimension of depth in all of them. Religion is the aspect of depth in the totality of the human spirit.

What does the metaphor *depth* mean? It means that the religious aspect points to that which is ultimate, infinite, unconditional in man's spiritual life. Religion, in the largest and most basic sense of the word, is ultimate concern. And ultimate concern is manifest in all creative functions of the human spirit. It is manifest in the moral sphere as the unconditional seriousness of the moral demand. Therefore, if someone rejects religion in the name of the moral function of the human spirit, he rejects religion in the name of religion. Ultimate concern is manifest in the realm of knowledge as the passionate longing for ultimate reality. Therefore, if anyone rejects religion in the name of the cognitive function of the human spirit, he rejects religion in the name of religion. Ultimate concern is manifest in the aesthetic function of the human spirit as the infinite desire to express ultimate meaning. Therefore, if anyone rejects religion in the name of the aesthetic function of the human spirit, he rejects religion in the name of religion. You cannot reject religion with ultimate seriousness, because ultimate seriousness, or the state of being ultimately concerned, is itself religion. Religion is the substance, the ground, and the depth of man's spiritual life. This is the religious aspect of the human spirit.

But now the question arises, what about religion in the narrower and customary sense of the word, be it institutional religion or the religion of personal piety? If religion is present in all functions of the spiritual life, why has mankind developed religion as a special sphere among others, in myth, cult, devotion, and ecclesiastical institutions? The answer is, because of the tragic estrangement of man's spiritual life from its own ground and depth. According to the visionary who has written the last book of the Bible, there will be no temple in the heavenly Jerusalem, for God will be all in all. There will be no secular realm, and for this very reason there will be no religious realm. Religion will be again what it is essentially, the all-determining ground and substance of man's spiritual life.

Religion opens up the depth of man's spiritual life which is usually covered by the dust of our daily life and the noise of our secular work. It gives us the experience of the Holy, of something which is untouchable, awe-inspiring, an ultimate meaning, the source of ultimate courage. This is the glory of what we call religion. But beside its glory lies its shame. It makes itself the ultimate and despises the secular realm. It makes its myths and doctrines, its rites and laws into ultimates and persecutes those who do not subject themselves to it. It forgets that its own existence is a result of man's tragic estrangement from his true being. It forgets its own emergency character.

This is the reason for the passionate reaction of the secular world against religion, a reaction which has tragic consequences for the secular realm itself. For the religious and the secular realm are in the same predicament. Neither of them should be in separation from the other, and both should realize that their very existence as separated is an emergency, that both of them are rooted in religion in the larger sense of the word, in the experience of ultimate concern. To the degree in which this is realized the conflicts between the religious and the secular are overcome, and religion has rediscovered its true place in man's spiritual life, namely, in its depth, out of which it gives substance, ultimate meaning, judgment, and creative courage to all functions of the human spirit.

II

The Two Types of Philosophy of Religion

ONE can distinguish two ways of approaching God: the way of overcoming estrangement and the way of meeting a stranger. In the first way man discovers *himself* when he discovers God; he discovers something that is identical with himself although it transcends him infinitely, something from which he is estranged, but from which he never has been and never can be separated. In the second way man meets a *stranger* when he meets God. The meeting is accidental. Essentially they do not belong to each other. They may become friends on a tentative and conjectural basis. But there is no certainty about the stranger man has met. He may disappear, and only *probable* statements can be made about his nature.

The two ways symbolize the two possible types of philosophy of religion: the ontological type and the cosmological type. The way of overcoming estrangement symbolizes the ontological method in the philosophy of religion. The way of meeting a stranger symbolizes the cosmological method. It is the purpose of this essay to show: (1) that the ontological method is basic for every philosophy of religion, (2) that the cosmological method without the ontological as its basis leads to a destructive cleavage between philosophy and religion, and (3) that on the basis of the ontological approach and with a dependent use of the cosmological way, philosophy of religion contributes to the reconciliation between religion and secular culture. These three points shall be discussed on the basis of extensive references to the classic expressions of the two types of philosophy of religion in the 13th century.

I. THE WORLD HISTORICAL PROBLEM

In two developments Western humanity has overcome its age-old bondage under the "powers": those half religious-half magical, half divine-half demonic, half superhuman-half subhuman, half abstract-half concrete beings who are the genuine material of the mythos. These "powers" were conquered *religiously* by their subjection to one of them, the god of the prophets of Israel; his quality as the god of justice enabled him to become the universal God. The "powers" were conquered *philosophically* by their subjection to a principle more real than all of them; its quality as embracing all qualities enabled it to become the universal principle. In this process the "powers" lost their sacred character and with it their hold on the human consciousness. All holiness was transferred to the absolute God or to the absolute principle. The gods disappeared and became servants of the absolute God, or appearances of the absolute principle. But the "powers," although subjected and transformed, were not extinguished. They could and can return and establish a reign of superstition and fear; and even the absolute God can become *one* power beside others, perhaps the highest, but not the absolute. It is one of the tasks of the philosophy of religion to protect religion as well as the scientific interpretation of reality against the return of the "powers" who threaten both at the same time.

The problem created by the subjection of the "powers" to the absolute God and to the absolute principle is *"the problem of the two Absolutes."* How are they related to each other? The religious and the philosophical Absolutes, *Deus* and *esse* cannot be unconnected! What is their connection from the point of view of being as well as of knowing? In the simple statement "God *is,*" the connection is achieved; but the character of this connection is *the* problem in all problems of the philosophy of religion. The different answers given to this question are milestones on the road of Western religious consciousness; and this road is a road towards ever-increasing *loss* of religious consciousness. Philosophy of religion, although not primarily responsible for this development, must ask itself whether according to its principles this was an unavoidable development and whether a reversal is possible.

II. THE AUGUSTINIAN SOLUTION

Augustine, after he had experienced all the implications of ancient scepticism, gave a classical answer to the problem of the two Absolutes: They coincide in the nature of truth. *Veritas* is presupposed in every philosophical argument; and *veritas* is God. You cannot deny truth as such because you could do it only in the name of truth, thus establishing truth. And if you establish truth you affirm God. "Where I have found the truth, there I have found my God, the truth itself," Augustine says. The question of the two Ultimates is solved in such a way that the religious Ultimate is presupposed in every philosophical question, including the question of God. *God is the presupposition of the question of God:* This is the ontological solution of the problem of the philosophy of religion. God can never be reached if he is the *object* of a question, and not its *basis.*

The Franciscan school of 13th-century scholasticism, represented by Alexander of Hales, Bonaventura, and Matthew of Aquasparta developed the Augustinian solution into a doctrine of the principles of theology, and maintained, in spite of some Aristotelian influences, the ontological type of the philosophy of religion. Their whole emphasis was on the immediacy of the knowledge of God. According to Bonaventura, "God is most truly present to the very soul and immediately knowable"; He is knowable in Himself without media as the one which is common to all. For He is the principle of knowledge, the first truth, in the light of which everything else is known, as Matthew says. As such He is the identity of subject and object. He is not subjected to doubt, which is possible only if subjectivity and objectivity are separated. Psychologically, of course, doubt is possible; but logically, the Absolute is affirmed by the very act of doubt, because it is implied in every statement about the relation between subject and predicate. *Ecce tibi est ipsa veritas. Amplectere illam.* (Thine is truth itself; embrace it.) These ultimate principles and knowledge of them are independent of the changes and relativities of the individual mind; they are the unchangeable, eternal light, appearing in the logical and mathematical axioms as well as in the first categories of thought. These principles are not created functions *of* our mind, but the presence of truth itself and therefore of God, *in* our mind. The Thomistic method of knowledge through sense perception and abstraction may be useful for scientific purposes, but it never can reach the Absolute. Anticipating the consequent development Matthew says about the Aristotelian-Thomistic approach: "For even if this method builds the way of science, it utterly destroys the way of wisdom." Wisdom, *sapientia*, is the knowledge of the principles, of truth itself. And this knowledge is either immediate or it is non-existent. It is distinguished from *humana rationatio*, human reasoning, as well as from *scripturarum autoritas*, the authority of the Holy Scripture. It is *certitudo ex se ipsis*, certainty out of the things themselves, without a medium. Perceiving and accepting the eternal truth are identical, as Alexander of Hales states.

The truth which is presupposed in every question and in every doubt precedes the cleavage into subject and object. Neither of them is an ultimate power. But they participate in the ultimate power above them, in Being itself, in *primum esse*. "Being is what first appears in the intellect" (*Quod primum cadit in intellectu*). And this Being (which is not *a* being) is pure actuality and therefore divine. We always see it, but we do not always notice it; as we see everything in the light without always noticing the light as such.

According to Augustine and his followers the *verum ipsum* is also the *bonum ipsum* because nothing which is less than the ultimate power of Being can be the ultimate power of good. No changeable or conditioned good can overcome the fear that it may be lost. Only in the Unchangeable can be found the *prius* of all goodness. In relation to *esse ipsum* no difference between the cognitive and the appetitive is possible, because a separation of the functions presupposes a separation of subject and object.

The Augustinian tradition can rightly be called mystical, if mysticism is defined as the experience of the identity of subject and object in relation to Being itself. In terms of our ideas of stranger and estrangement, Meister Eckart says: "There is between God and the soul neither strangeness nor remoteness, therefore the soul is not only equal with God but it is . . . the same that He is." This is, of course, a paradoxical statement, as Eckart and all mystics knew; for in order to *state* the identity, an element of non-identity must be presupposed. This proved to be the dynamic and critical point in the ontological approach.

On this basis the ontological argument for the existence of God must be understood. It is neither an argument, nor does it deal with the existence of God, although it often has been expressed in this form. It is the rational description of the relation of our mind to Being as such. Our mind implies *principia per se nota* which have immediate evidence whenever they are noticed: the transcendentalia, *esse, verum, bonum.* They constitute the Absolute in which the difference between knowing and known is not actual. This Absolute as the principle of Being has absolute certainty. It is a necessary thought because it is the presupposition of all thought. "The divine substance is known in such a way that it cannot be thought not to be," says Alexander of Hales. The fact that people turn away from this thought is based on individual defects but not on the essential structure of the mind. The mind is able to turn away from what is nearest to the ground of its own structure. This is the nerve of the ontological argument. But Anselm, on the basis of his epistemological realism, transformed the *primum esse* into an *ens realissimum*, the principle into a universal being. In doing so he was open to all attacks, from Gaunilo and Thomas to Kant, who rightly deny that there is a logical transition from the necessity of Being itself to a highest being, from a principle which is beyond essence and existence to something that exists.

But even in this insufficient form the meaning of the ontological answer to the question of the two Absolutes is visible. *Deus est esse*, and the certainty of God is identical with the certainty of Being itself: God is the presupposition of the question of God.

III. THE THOMISTIC DISSOLUTION

The ontological approach as elaborated by Augustine and his school had led to difficulties, as they appeared in the Anselmian form of the ontological argument and in the theological use of it by the great Franciscans. Here the criticism of Aquinas starts. But this criticism in Thomas himself and more radically in Duns Scotus and William of Occam, goes far beyond the abuses and difficulties. It has, for the larger part of Western humanity, undermined the ontological approach and with it the immediate religious certainty. It has replaced the first type of philosophy of religion by the second type.

The general character of the Thomistic approach to the philosophy of religion is the following: The rational way to God is not immediate, but mediated. It is a way of inference which, although correct, does not give unconditional certainty; therefore it must be completed by the way of authority. This means that the immediate rationality of the Franciscans is replaced by an argumentative rationality, and that beside this rational element stands non-rational authority. In order to make this step, Thomas had to dismiss the Augustinian solution. So he says: "There are two ways in which something is known: by itself and by us. Therefore I say that this proposition 'God is' is known by itself insofar as He is *in* Himself, because the predicate is the same as the subject. For God is His own being . . . But since *we* do not know about God, what He is, that proposition is not known by itself, but must be demonstrated through those things which are more known with respect to us, that is, through His effects." In these words Aquinas cuts the nerve of the ontological approach. Man is excluded from the *primum esse* and the *prima veritas*. It is impossible for him to adhere to the uncreated truth. For the principles, the transcendentalia, are *not* the presence of the divine in us, they are *not* the "uncreated light" through which we see everything, but they are the created structure of our mind. It is obvious that in this way the immediate knowledge of the Absolute is destroyed. *Sapientia*, the knowledge of the principles, is qualitatively not different from *scientia*. As a student of music has to accept the propositions of the mathematicians, even if he does not understand their full meaning, so man has to accept the propositions of that science which God has of Himself and which the angels fully undersand. They are given us by authority. "Arguing out of authority is most appropriate to this doctrine (theology)," Thomas says. The Bible, consequently, becomes a collection of true propositions, instead of being a guide book to contemplation as in Bonaventura. And while the Franciscans, especially Alexander, distinguish between (a) those doctrines which belong to the eternal truth and are immediately evident, (as for instance, God as *esse, verum, bonum*) and (b) those doctrines which are secondary, embodying the eternal truth in temporal forms, and are contingent and not evident, (as for instance, the Incarnation and the doctrine of the Church), Thomas puts all theological statements on the same level, namely that of authority. This has the consequence that *credere* and *intelligere* are torn asunder. According to Thomas the same object cannot be the object of faith and of knowledge; for faith does not imply an immediate contact with its object. Faith is less than knowledge. "So far as vision is lacking to it, faith falls short of the order of knowledge which is present in science," says Thomas; and vision, according to him, is not possible in our bodily existence. Here are the roots of that deteriorization of the term "faith" by which it is understood as belief with a low degree of evidence and which makes its use today almost impossible. The separation of faith in the sense of subjection to authority, and knowledge in the sense of science, entails the separation of the psychological functions which in Augustine are expressions of the same psychic substance. The intellect is moved by the will to accept contents which are accidental to the intellect; without the command of the will, assent to the transcendent science cannot be reached. The will fills the gap which the intellect cannot bridge, after the ontological immediacy has been taken away.

For Thomas all this follows from his sense-bound epistemology: "The human intellect cannot reach by natural virtue the divine substance, because, according to the way of the present life the cognition of our intellect starts with the senses." From there we must ascend to God with the help of the category of causality. This is what the philosophy of religion can do, and can do fairly easily in cosmological terms. We can see that there must be pure actuality, since the movement from potentiality to actuality is dependent on actuality, so that an actuality, preceding every movement, must exist. The ontological argument is impossible, not only in its doubtful form, but in its very substance. Gilson puts it this way: "It is indeed incontestable that in God essence and existence are identical. But this is true of the existence in which God subsists eternally in Himself; not of the existence to which our finite mind can rise when, by demonstration, it establishes that God is." It is obvious that this second concept of existence brings God's existence down to the level of that of a stone or a star, and it makes atheism not only possible, but almost unavoidable, as the later development has proved.

The first step in this direction was taken by Duns Scotus, who asserted an insuperable gap between man as finite and God as the infinite being, and who derived from this separation that the cosmological arguments as *demonstrationes ex finito* remain within the finite and cannot reach the infinite. They cannot transcend the idea of a self-moving, teleological universe. Only authority can go beyond this rational probability of God which is a mere possibility. The concept of being loses its ontological character; it is a word, covering the entirely different realms of the finite and the infinite. God ceases to be Being itself and becomes a particular being, who must be known, *cognitione particulari*. Occam, the father of later nominalism, calls God a *res singularissima*. He can be approached neither by intuition nor by abstraction; that means not at all, except through an unnoticeable habit of grace in the unconscious which is supposed to move the will towards subjection to authority. This is the final outcome of the Thomistic *dis*solution of the Augustinian *solution*. The question of the two Ultimates is answered in such a way that the religious Absolute has become a singular being of over-whelming power, while the philosophical Absolute is formalized into a given structure of reality in which everything is contingent and individual. Early Protestantism was rather wise when under these philosophical presuppositions it restrained itself from developing any philosophy of religion, and elaborated in the power of its religious experience a concept of faith in which the disrupted elements of later scholasticism entered a new synthesis. For this was the gain of the Thomistic turn, that the nature of faith was thoroughly discussed and the naive identification of immediate evidence with faith was overcome, so that the contingent element in religion became visible.

IV. CONFLICTS AND MIXTURES OF THE TWO TYPES IN THE MODERN PHILOSOPHY OF RELIGION

The material which could be collected under this heading is immense. But its originality, in comparison with the classical answers, is small. These answers return again and again, separated or in mixture. While the general trend is determined by the cosmological type and its final self-negation, ontological reactions against it occur in all centuries and have become more frequent in recent years.

It has often been said that the moral type of philosophy of religion (which follows Kant's so-called moral argument for the existence of God) represents a new type. But this is not the case. The moral argument must be either interpreted cosmologically or ontologically. If it is understood cosmologically, the fact of moral valuation is the basis of an inference, leading to a highest being who guarantees the ultimate unity of value and perfection or to the belief in the victorious power of value-creating processes. If the moral argument is interpreted in the ontological way, the experience of the unconditional character of the moral command is immediately, without any inference, the awareness of the Absolute, though not of a highest being. It is interesting to notice in this connection that even the ontological argument can be formulated cosmologically, as for instance, when Descartes, following Duns Scotus, makes an inference from the idea of an infinite being in our mind to his existence as the cause of this idea. This is the basic difference between the Augustinian and Cartesian starting point; it is rooted in the removal of the mystical element of Augustine's idea of ultimate evidence by Descartes' concept of rationality.

Obviously, German idealism belongs to the ontological

type of philosophy of religion. It was not wrong in re-
establishing the *prius* of subject and object, but it was wrong
in deriving from the Absolute the whole of contingent contents, an attempt from which the Franciscans were protected
by their religious positivism. This overstepping of the limits
of the ontological approach has discredited it in Protestantism,
while the same mistake of the neo-scholastic ontologists has
discredited it in Catholicism.

No new type has been produced by the so-called empirical
or experimental philosophy of religion. Most of its representatives belong to the cosmological type. They argue for God as
"the best explanation of man's general experiences" or for
"the theistic hypothesis" as the "most reasonable belief," etc.
in innumerable variations; adding to it, as the cosmological
type always must, remnants of the Old-Protestant idea of
personal faith, which remain unrelated to the cosmological
probabilities. Often, however, an idea of religious experience
is used which has little in common with an empirical approach, and uses Franciscan terms and assertions. If the idea
of God is to be formulated "in such a way that the question
of God's existence becomes a dead issue" (Wieman); if
Lyman speaks of "the innermost center of man which is in
kinship with the Deepest Reality in the Universe"; if Baillie
denies the possibility of genuine atheism; if the concept of
vision is used again and again, for our knowledge of God, we
are in an ontological atmosphere, although the ontological
approach is not clearly stated and its relation to the cosmological approach and to faith is not adequately explained.

More consciously ontological are philosophies of religion
like that of Hocking, who emphasizes the immediate experience of "Wholeness" as the *prius* of all objective knowledge
with respect to being and value, or of Whitehead who calls
the primordial nature of God the principle of concretion, or

of Hartshorne, who tries to re-establish the ontological argument and to combine it with the "contingent" in God. With respect to genuine pragmatism, it belongs to the ontological line in so far as it clearly rejects the cosmological argumentation and refuses to accept the cleavage between subject and object as final. It is, however, not free from remnants of the cosmological type, as James's Scotistic doctrine of the "will to believe," and the widespread assumption that the end of the cosmological way is the end of any rational approach to religion, indicate.

The systematic solution here suggested is stated in a merely affirmative and constructive form. The arguments on which this systematic attempt is based are implied in the classical discussion of the two ways of a philosophy of religion and its modern repercussions. They clearly show why, after the destruction of the ontological approach, religion itself was destroyed.

V. THE ONTOLOGICAL AWARENESS OF THE UNCONDITIONAL

The question of the two Absolutes can be answered only by the identification of the philosophical Absolute with the *one* element of the religious Absolute. The *Deus est esse* is the basis of all philosophy of religion. It is the condition of a unity between thought and religion which overcomes their, so to speak, schizophrenic cleavages in personal and cultural life.

The ontological principle in the philosophy of religion may be stated in the following way: *Man is immediately aware of something unconditional which is the prius of the separation and interaction of subject and object, theoretically as well as practically.*

Awareness, in this proposition, is used as the most neutral term, avoiding the connotations of the terms intuition, experience, knowledge. Awareness of the Unconditioned has not the character of "intuition," for the Unconditioned does not appear in this awareness as a *"Gestalt"* to be intuited, but as an element, a power, as demand. Thomas was right in denying that the vision of God is a human possibility, in so far as men in time and space are concerned. Neither should the word "experience" be used, because it ordinarily describes the observed presence of one reality to another reality, and because the Unconditioned is not a matter of experiential observation. "Knowledge" finally presupposes the separation of subject and object, and implies an isolated theoretical act, which is just the opposite of awareness of the Unconditioned. But this terminological question is not of primary importance. It is obvious that the ontological awareness is immediate, and not mediated by inferential processes. It is present, whenever conscious attention is focussed on it, in terms of an unconditional certainty.

Awareness, of course, is also a cognitive term. But awareness of the Unconditional is itself unconditional, and therefore beyond the division of the psychological functions. It was a main interest of Augustinian psychology to show the mutual immanence of the functions of the soul and the impossibility of separating them in their relation to the *esse, verum, bonum*. It is impossible to be aware of the Unconditioned as if it did not exclude by its very presence any observer who was not conditioned by it in his whole being. Thomas injured the understanding of religion when he dissolved the substantial unity of the psychological functions, and attributed to the will in isolation what the intellect alone is not able to perform. And Schleiermacher injured the understanding of religion when in his great fight against the cosmological approach of Protestant Enlightenment he cut "feeling" (as the religious function) off from will and intellect, thus excluding religion from the totality of personal existence and delivering it to emotional subjectivity. *Man*, not his cognitive function alone, is aware of the Unconditioned. It would therefore be possible to call this awareness "existential" in the sense in which Existential philosophy has used the word, namely the participation of man as a whole in the cognitive act. In fact, this is probably the only point where this term could adequately be used in philosophy. The reason it is not used here is the essential unity of the unconditional and the conditioned in the ontological awareness; while in the word "existential," separation and decision are indicated. And the latter are elements of faith. While theology is directly and intentionally existential, philosophy is so only indirectly and unintentionally through the existential situation of the philosopher.

The term "unconditional" needs some interpretation. Although in the historical part the phrase "the two Absolutes" is applied, in order to explain the problem, the word is replaced by "unconditional" in the constructive part. "Absolute," if taken literally, means "without relation"; if taken traditionally, it connotes the idealistic, self-developing principle. Both meanings are avoided in the concept "unconditional," which implies the unconditional demand upon those who are aware of something unconditional, and which cannot be interpreted as the principle of a rational deduction. But even here wrong connotations must be prevented: Neither "The Unconditioned" nor "something unconditional," is meant as a being, not even the highest being, not even God. God is unconditioned, that makes him God; but the "unconditional" is not God. The word "God" is filled with the concrete symbols in which mankind has expressed its ultimate concern—its being grasped by something unconditional. And this "something" is not just a thing, but the power of being in which every being participates.

This power of being is the *prius* of everything that has being. It precedes all special contents logically and ontologically. It precedes every separation and makes every interaction possible, because it is the point of identity without which neither separation nor interaction can be thought. This refers basically to the separation and interaction of subject and object, in knowing as well as in acting. The *prius* of subject and object cannot become an object to which man as a subject is theoretically and practically related. God is no object for us as subjects. He is always that which precedes this division. But, on the other hand, we speak about him and we act upon him, and we cannot avoid it, because everything which becomes real to us enters the subject-object correlation. Out of this paradoxical situation the half-blasphemous and mythological concept of the "existence of God" has arisen. And so have the abortive attempts to prove the existence of this "object." To such a concept and to such attempts atheism is the right religious and theological reply. This was well known to the most intensive piety of all times. The atheistic terminology of mysticism is striking. It leads beyond God to the Unconditioned, transcending any fixation of the divine as an object. But we have the same feeling of the inadequacy of all limiting names for God in non-mystical religion. Genuine religion without an element of atheism cannot be imagined. It is not by chance that not only Socrates, but also the Jews and the early Christians were persecuted as atheists. For those who adhered to the powers, they were atheists.

The ontological approach transcends the discussion between nominalism and realism, if it rejects the concept of the *ens realissimum*, as it must do. Being itself, as present in the ontological awareness, is power of Being but not the most powerful being; it is neither *ens realissimum* nor *ens singularissimum*. It is the power in everything that has power, be it a universal or an individual, a thing or an experience.

VI. THE COSMOLOGICAL RECOGNITION OF THE UNCONDITIONED

History and analysis have shown that the cosmological approach to religion leads to the self-destruction of religion, except as it is based on the ontological approach. If this basis is given, the cosmological principle can be stated in the following way: *The Unconditioned of which we have an immediate awareness, without inference, can be recognized in the cultural and natural universe.*

The cosmological approach has usually appeared in two forms, the first determined by the cosmological and the second by the teleological argument. After having denied radically the argumentative method applied in this kind of cosmology, we can rediscover the real and extremely productive meaning of the cosmological way in the philosophy of religion. From two points of view this can be done and has to be done, more than ever since the Franciscan period, in the last decades of our time. The one kind of cosmological recognition follows the first step of the old cosmological argument, namely the analysis of the finitude of the finite in the light of the awareness of the Unconditioned. In concepts like contingency, insecurity, transitoriness, and their psychological correlates anxiety, care, meaninglessness, a new cosmological approach has developed. Medical psychology, the doctrine of man, and the Existential philosophy have con-

tributed to this negative way of recognizing the unconditional element in man and his world. It is the most impressive
way of introducing people into the meaning of religion—if
the fallacious inference to a highest being is avoided.

The other kind of cosmological recognition is affirmative
and follows the first step of the teleological argument, namely, the tracing of the unconditional element in the creativity
of nature and culture. With respect to nature this has been
done in the elaboration and ultimate valuation of ideas such
as "wholeness," "*élan vital*," "principle of concretion," "*Gestalt*," etc., in all of which something unconditional, condition-
ing any special experience, is implied. With respect to culture
this has been done by a religious interpretation of the autonomous culture and its development, a "theology of culture"
as it could be called. The presupposition of this many-sided
attempt is that in every cultural creation—a picture, a system,
a law, a political movement (however secular it may appear)
—an ultimate concern is expressed, and that it is possible to
recognize the unconscious theological character of it.

This, of course, is possible only on the basis of the ontological awareness of the Unconditioned, i.e. on the basis of the
insight that secular culture is essentially as impossible as
atheism, because both presuppose the unconditional element
and both express ultimate concerns.

VII. ONTOLOGICAL CERTAINTY AND THE RISK OF FAITH

The immediate awareness of the Unconditioned has not the
character of faith but of self-evidence. Faith contains a contingent element and demands a risk. It combines the ontologi-

cal certainty of the Unconditioned with the uncertainty about everything conditioned and concrete. This, of course, does not mean that faith is belief in something which has higher or lower degrees of probability. The risk of faith is not that it accepts assertions about God, man and world, which cannot be fully verified, but might be or might not be in the future. The risk of faith is based on the fact that the unconditional element can become a matter of ultimate concern only if it appears in a concrete embodiment. It can appear in purified and rationalized mythological symbols like God as highest personal being, and like most of the other traditional theological concepts. It can appear in ritual and sacramental activities for the adherents of a priestly and authoritarian religion. It can appear in concrete formulas and a special behavior, expressing the ineffable, as it always occurs in living mysticism. It can appear in prophetic-political demands for social justice, if they are the ultimate concern of religious and secular movements. It can occur in the honesty and ultimate devotion of the servants of scientific truth. It can occur in the universalism of the classical idea of personality and in the Stoic (ancient and modern) attitude of elevation over the vicissitudes of existence. In all these cases the risk of faith is an existential risk, a risk in which the meaning and fulfilment of our lives is at stake, and not a theoretical judgment which may be refuted sooner or later.

The risk of faith is not arbitrariness; it is a unity of fate and decision. And it is based on a foundation which is not risk: the awareness of the unconditional element in ourselves and our world. Only on this basis is faith justified and possible. There are many examples of people of the mystical as well as of the prophetic and secular types who in moments (and even periods) of their lives experienced the failure of the faith they had risked, and who preserved the ontological certainty, the unconditional element in their faith. The profoundest doubt could not undermine the presupposition of doubt, the awareness of something unconditional.

Although faith is a matter of fate and decision, the question must be raised whether there is a criterion for the element of decision in faith. The answer is: The unconditional of which we are immediately aware, if we turn our minds to it. The criterion of every concrete expression of our ultimate concern is the degree to which the concreteness of the concern is in unity with its ultimacy. It is the danger of every embodiment of the unconditional element, religious and secular, that it elevates something conditioned, a symbol, an institution, a movement as such to ultimacy. This danger was well known to the religious leaders of all types; and the whole work of theology can be summed up in the statement, that it is the permanent guardian of the unconditional against the aspiration of its own religious and secular appearances.

The ontological approach to philosophy of religion as envisaged by Augustine and his followers, as reappearing in many forms in the history of thought, if critically reinterpreted by us, is able to do for our time what it did in the past, both for religion and culture: to overcome as far as it is possible by mere thought the fateful gap between religion and culture, thus reconciling concerns which are not strange to each other but have been estranged from each other.

III

The Struggle Between
Time and Space

TIME and space should be treated as struggling forces, as living beings, as subjects with power of their own. This of course, is a way of speaking, but it is a way which I think is justified by the fact that time and space are the main structures of existence to which all existing things, the whole finite realm, are subjected. Existing means being finite or being in time and space. This holds true of everything in our world. Time and space are the powers of universal existence including human existence, human body and mind. Time and space belong together: We can measure time only by space and space only in time. Motion, the universal character of life, needs time and space. Mind, which seems to be bound to time, needs only embodiment in order to come to existence, and consequently it needs space.

But while time and space are bound to each other in such an inescapable way, they stand in a tension with each other which may be considered as the most fundamental tension of existence. In the human mind, this tension becomes conscious and gets historical power. Human soul and human history, to a large extent, are determined by the struggle between space and time.

It is extremely interesting but it would lead too far to consider at length the struggle between space and time in nature itself: The entire control of time and space in the realm of mathematical physics, in which time for the purpose of calculation can be used as the fourth dimension of space, and the physical process can be turned around whereby time is deprived of its most essential quality—to have a direction. Time without direction is time under the full control of space. Therefore, it is the first victory of time that the process of life goes from birth to death, that growth and decay create a direction which cannot be reversed. The aged cannot become young again in the realm of life. Nevertheless, the predominance of space remains. The life-process cannot be reversed, but it can be repeated. Each individual life repeats the law of birth and death, of growth and decay. The direction of time is deprived of its power by the circular motion of continuous repetition. The circle, this most expressive symbol of the predominance of space, is not overcome in the realm of life.

In man the final victory of time is possible. Man is able to act towards something beyond his death. He is able to have history, and he is able to transcend even the tragic death of families and nations, thus breaking through the circle of repetition towards something new. Because he is able to do so, he represents the potential victory of time, but not always the actual victory. What has happened in nature unconsciously happens in man and history consciously: The same struggle and the same victory.

SPACE AND NATIONALISM

Paganism can be defined as the elevation of a special space to ultimate value and dignity. Paganism has a god who is bound to one place beside and against other places. Therefore, paganism necessarily is polytheistic. Polytheism does not mean that a group of people believes in several gods, as monotheism does not mean the belief in one God only. The difference is not a difference of number but of quality. Only if the one God is exclusively God, unconditioned and unlimited by anything other than Himself, is there a true monotheism, and only then is the power of space over time broken.

The power of space is great, and it is always active both for creation and destruction. It is the basis of the desire of any group of human beings to have a place of their own, a place which gives them reality, presence, power of living, which feeds them, body and soul. This is the reason for the adoration of earth and soil, not of soil generally but of this special soil, and not of earth generally but of the divine powers connected with this special section of the earth. But there are many soils and many sections of the earth and each of them has creative force for some group of people, and consequently claims divine honor by this group. Divine honor means ultimate honor, unconditioned adoration, because the divine, by its very definition, is ultimate, unlimited power. But every space is limited, and so the conflict arises between the limited space of any human group, even of mankind itself, and the unlimited claim which follows from the deification of this space. The god of the one country struggles with the god of the other country, for every spatial god is imperialistic by his very character of being a god. The law of mutual destruction, therefore, is the unavoidable fate of the powers of space.

Space means more than a piece of soil. It includes everything which has the character of "beside-each-otherness." Examples of spatial concepts are blood and race, clan, tribe, and family. We know how powerful the gods are who give ultimate dignity and value to a special race and to a special community of blood. In all of them the "beside-each-otherness" is dominating. Human culture is rooted in these realities, and it is not surprising that they always have received adoration, consciously and unconsciously, by those who belong to them, and consequently that they always have claimed universal validity.

Modern nationalism is the actual form in which space is ruling over time, in which polytheism is a daily reality. Nobody can deny the tremendous creativity of national community. Nobody would be willing to deprive himself of the physical and psychological space which is his nation. Nobody would do so or ever did so, without suffering and loss. But on the other hand, our generation has experienced again and again the most terrifying mutual destruction of the space-centered powers. The "beside-each-otherness" necessarily becomes an "against-each-otherness" in the moment in which a special space gets divine honor. And this is the case in all nationalism throughout the world, not only in those countries which try to reintroduce religious symbols and cults for their nationalistic pagan creed.

SPACE, TRAGEDY, AND MYSTICISM

Human existence under the predominance of space is tragic. Greek tragedy and philosophy knew about this. They knew that the Olympic gods were gods of space, one beside the other, one struggling with the other. Even Zeus was only the first of many equals, and hence subject, together with man and the other gods, to the tragic law of genesis and decay. Greek tragedy, philosophy, and art were wrestling with the tragic law of our spatial existence. They were seeking for an immovable being beyond the circle of genesis and decay, greatness and self-destruction, something beyond tragedy.

But the power of space was overwhelming in Greek mind

and existence. The ultimate symbol found by Greek philosophy for the immovable being is the sphere or the circle, the most perfect representation of space. If you look at classical sculpture or at the archaic temples in Sicily and Paestum, you must feel immediately that they are enclosed in a sphere. They have no dynamic trend to go beyond it. They are in space, fulfilling it with divine force, bound to their space, expressing the tragic limitation of it. Greek reason never was able to overcome this limitation. Even the logic of Aristotle is a spatial logic, unable to express the dynamic trend of time. There is no philosophy of history in Greek thought, and where history is dealt with it is considered as only a section of the long circular motion of the whole cosmos from birth to death, of one world replacing the other. Time is swallowed by space in this cosmological tragedy.

It is understandable that finally the Greek mind tried to escape the tragic circle of genesis and decay by escaping reality completely. It is understandable that the last task of Greek philosophy was mysticism, trying the way of the Asiatic religions and cultures. So we have to ask: What about time and space in mysticism? The answer is: Mysticism is no real escape from the predominance of space. It extinguishes time and space, but in so doing, it maintains the basic presupposition that time cannot create something entirely new, that everything in time is subject to the circle of birth and death, and that no new creature can arise. Therefore, salvation is beyond time, it is always independent of any stage of time. It is the eternal present above every temporal present.

Mysticism is the most subtle form of the predominance of space. It is the most subtle form of denying history, but in denying the meaning of history, it denies the meaning of time. Mysticism is the spiritual form of the power of space over time, and therefore we can say that mysticism, in the sense of the great mystics, is the most sublime form of poly-theism. In the abyss of the Eternal One, of Atman-Brahman, of the Pure Nothing, of the Nirvana, or whatever the names of this nameless one may be, all individual gods and their spaces disappear. But they only disappear, and therefore they can return. They are not overcome in time and history. And the history of religion shows that in the later ancient period, as well as in later Buddhism and Hinduism, polytheism returned. It was a very much weakened form of polytheism. The single gods were not taken quite seriously. It was a soaring between space and the negation of space, but it was not the affirmation of time. Supernature as well as nature subjects time to space.

TIME AND THE PROPHETIC MESSAGE

The turning point in the struggle between space and time in history is the prophetic message. To the birth of man out of nature and against nature corresponds the birth of prophetism out of paganism and against paganism.

This birth is symbolized in the story of the vocation of Abraham. The command to Abraham to leave his homeland and his father's house means the command to leave the gods of soil and blood, of family, tribe and nation; that is, the gods of space, the gods of paganism and polytheism, the gods who stand beside each other—even if one of them is the most powerful. The true God who spoke to Abraham cannot be identified with a family or city-god. In the moment in which the danger of such an identification arises, God must separate Himself from those who adore Him. The representative of this separation is the prophet. He does not deny the God of the fathers, but he protests against the abuse of this God by the priests of soil and blood, of tribe and nation. He pronounces the separation of God from His nation. This becomes obvious in the great prophets who announce the complete rejection of the nation by God if it continues as a pagan cult with pagan ethics and politics.

The threat which we hear first in the words of Amos is the turning point in the history of religion. It is unheard of in all other religions that the God of a nation is able to destroy this nation without being destroyed Himself. In all other religions the god dies with the people who adore him. In prophetism the glory of God is not diminished, but augmented by the split between God and nation. This, and this alone, is the end of polytheism. A struggle against the gods of space was made by those prophets who destroyed the places of adoration all over the country, thereby cutting off the roots of pagan revivalism and concentrating the cult in Jerusalem. And when Jerusalem fell, the power of the God of time was strong enough to survive this greatest of all catastrophies, and to become the God of the world before whom the nations are like the sand of the sea. This was a triumph unimaginable in all paganism, and was due to the principle of separation implied in the command to Abraham.

And in the period of the New Testament, the message that God must be adored neither in a temple nor on a mountain, but in Spirit and in Truth fulfills the prophetic message. But when this message became distorted by timeless gnosticism and mysticism, the Christian Church in one of its most vital struggles, overcame, in the name of the Old Testament, the temptation to become a group of timeless individuals bound not to a physical or psychological space, but to the spiritual timeless space of mysticism. And when Christianity became identified with the psychological space of a visible Church, and even more became subject to a physical space—the Roman priest—the Protestant protest renewed the prophetic negation of the gods of space. And when today a secularized Protestantism has produced the vacuum into which old pagan gods of soil and blood, race and nation are penetrating in all countries, there are still voices raised which indicate that the command to Abraham is not forgotten.

The God of time is the God of history. This means, first of all, that He is the God who acts in history towards a final goal. History has a direction, something new is to be created in it and through it. This goal is described in many different terms: universal blessedness, the victory over the demonic powers represented as imperialistic nations, the coming of the Kingdom of God in history and beyond history, the transformation of the form of this world, and so on. There are many symbols, some more immanent as in old prophetism and modern Protestantism, some more transcendent as in later apocalyptics and traditional Christianity, but in all these cases time is directing, creating, something new, a "new creature" as Paul calls it. The tragic circle of space is overcome. There is a definite beginning and a definite end in history.

History is universal history in prophetism. The limitations of space, the boundaries between nations are negated. In Abraham all nations shall be blessed, all nations shall adore on Mount Zion, the suffering of the elected nation has saving power for all nations. The miracle of Pentecost overcomes the cleavage between the languages. In Christ, the cosmos, the universe is saved and united. Missions have a universal claim trying to create an undivided human consciousness. Time is fulfilled in history, and history is fulfilled in the universal Kingdom of God, the Kingdom of justice and peace.

This leads to the ultimate point in the struggle between time and space. Prophetic monotheism is the monotheism of justice. The gods of space necessarily destroy justice. The unlimited claim of every spatial god unavoidably clashes with the unlimited claim of any other spatial god. The will to power of the one group cannot give justice to another group. This holds true of the powerful groups within a nation and of the nations themselves. Polytheism, the religion of space, is necessarily unjust. The unlimited claim of any god of space destroys the universalism implied in the idea of justice. This and this alone is the meaning of prophetic monotheism. God is one God because justice is one. The prophetic threat against the elected nation, that it will be rejected by God because of injustice, is the real victory over the gods of space. The interpretation of history in Deutero-Isaiah, according to which God calls the foreign nations in order to punish His own nation because of its injustice, elevates God to the universal God. Tragedy and injustice belong to the gods of space; historical fulfillment and justice belong to the God who acts in time and through time, uniting the separated space of his universe in love.

TIME AND JUDAISM

The Jewish nation is the nation of time in a sense which cannot be said of any other nation. It represents the permanent struggle between time and space going through all times. It can exist in spite of the loss of its space again and again, from the time of the great prophets, up to our days. It has a tragic fate when considered as a nation of space like every other nation, but as the nation of time, it is beyond tragedy. It is beyond tragedy because it is beyond the circle of life and death. The people of time in Synagogue and Church cannot avoid being persecuted because by their very existence, they break the claims of the gods of space who express themselves in will to power, imperialism, injustice, demonic enthusiasm, and tragic self-destruction. The gods of space who are strong in every human soul, in every race and nation, are afraid of the Lord of time, history, and justice, are afraid of His prophets and followers, and try to make them powerless and homeless. But just thereby these gods help to fulfill against their will the purpose of history and the meaning of time.

Christianity has separated from Judaism because in the fulfillment of time Judaism has made a decision for space, namely for its national law, which never could become the law of all nations. The assembly of God, namely the Church which gathers from all nations, is the end of all religious nationalism and tribalism, even if expressed in terms of prophetic traditions. On the other hand, the Church is always in danger of identifying herself with a national Church, or of leaving injustice, the will-to-power, national and racial arrogance unchallenged. The Church is always in danger of losing its prophetic spirit. Therefore, the prophetic spirit included in the traditions of the Synagogue is needed as long as the gods of time are in power, and this means up to the end of history, as Paul, the first Christian interpreter of the historical fate of Judaism, seems to assume in Romans 9–11.

Synagogue and Church should be united in our age, in the struggle for the God of time against the gods of space. This is a period in which more than ever since Christianity has overcome paganism the gods of space show their power over souls and nations. If this would happen, if all those who struggle for the Lord of history, for his justice and truth, are united even under persecution and martyrdom, the eternal victory in the struggle between time and space will become visible once more as the victory of time and the one God who is the Lord of history.

IV

Aspects of a Religious
Analysis of Culture

IF WE abstract the concept of religion from the great commandment, we can say that religion is being ultimately concerned about that which is and should be our ultimate concern. This means that faith is the state of being grasped by an ultimate concern, and God is the name for the content of the concern. Such a concept of religion has little in common with the description of religion as the belief in the existence of a highest being called God, and the theoretical and practical consequences of such a belief. Instead, we are pointing to an existential, not a theoretical, understanding of religion.

Christianity claims that the God who is manifest in Jesus the Christ is the true God, the true subject of an ultimate and unconditional concern. Judged by him, all other gods are less than valid objects of an ultimate concern, and if they are made into one, become idols. Christianity can claim this extraordinary character because of the extraordinary character of the events on which it is based, namely, the creation of a new reality within and under the conditions of man's predicament. Jesus as the bringer of this new reality is subject to those conditions, to finitude and anxiety, to law and tragedy, to conflicts and death. But he victoriously keeps the unity with God, sacrificing himself as Jesus to himself as the

Christ. In doing so he creates the new reality of which the Church is the communal and historical embodiment.

From this it follows that the unconditional claim made by Christianity is not related to the Christian Church, but to the event on which the Church is based. If the Church does not subject itself to the judgment which is pronounced by the Church, it becomes idolatrous towards itself. Such idolatry is its permanent temptation, just because it is the bearer of the New Being in history. As such it judges the world by its very presence. But the Church is also of the world and included under the judgment with which it judges the world. A Church which tries to exclude itself from such a judgment loses its right to judge the world and is rightly judged by the world. This is the tragedy of the Roman Catholic Church. Its way of dealing with culture is dependent upon its unwillingness to subject itself to the judgment pronounced by itself. Protestantism, at least in principle, resists this temptation, though actually it falls into it in many ways, again and again.

A second consequence of the existential concept of religion is the disappearance of the gap between the sacred and secular realm. If religion is the state of being grasped by an ultimate concern, this state cannot be restricted to a special realm. The unconditional character of this concern implies that it refers to every moment of our life, to every space and every realm. The universe is God's sanctuary. Every work day is a day of the Lord, every supper a Lord's supper, every work the fulfillment of a divine task, every joy a joy in God. In all preliminary concerns, ultimate concern is present, consecrating them. Essentially the religious and the secular are not separated realms. Rather they are within each other.

But this is not the way things actually are. In actuality, the secular element tends to make itself independent and to establish a realm of its own. And in opposition to this, the religious element tends to establish itself also as a special realm. Man's predicament is determined by this situation. It is the situation of the estrangement of man from his true being. One could rightly say that the existence of religion as a special realm is the most conspicuous proof of man's fallen state. This does not mean that under the conditions of estrangement which determine our destiny the religious should be swallowed by the secular, as secularism desires, nor that the secular should be swallowed by the religious, as ecclesiastic imperialism desires. But it does mean that the inseparable division is a witness to our human predicament.

The third consequence following from the existential concept of religion refers to the relation of religion and culture. Religion as ultimate concern is the meaning-giving substance of culture, and culture is the totality of forms in which the basic concern of religion expresses itself. In abbreviation: religion is the substance of culture, culture is the form of religion. Such a consideration definitely prevents the establishment of a dualism of religion and culture. Every religious act, not only in organized religion, but also in the most intimate movement of the soul, is culturally formed.

The fact that every act of man's spiritual life is carried by language, spoken or silent, is proof enough for this assertion. For language is the basic cultural creation. On the other hand, there is no cultural creation without an ultimate concern expressed in it. This is true of the theoretical functions of man's spiritual life, e.g. artistic intuition and cognitive reception of reality, and it is true of the practical functions of man's spiritual life, e.g. personal and social transformation of reality. In each of these functions in the whole of man's cultural creativity, an ultimate concern is present. Its immediate expression is the style of a culture. He who can read the style of a culture can discover its ultimate concern, its religious substance. This we will now try to do in relation . present culture.

THE SPECIAL CHARACTER OF CONTEMPORARY CULTURE

Our present culture must be described in terms of one predominant movement and an increasingly powerful protest against this movement. The spirit of the predominant movement is the spirit of industrial society. The spirit of the protest is the spirit of the existentialist analysis of man's actual predicament. The actual style of our life, as it was shaped in the 18th and 19th centuries, expresses the still unbroken power of the spirit of industrial society. There are numerous analyses of this style of thought, life, and artistic expression. One of the difficulties in analyzing it is its dynamic character, its continuous change, and the influence the protest against it has already had upon it. We may nevertheless elaborate two main characteristics of man in industrial society.

The first of these is the concentration of man's activities upon the methodical investigation and technical transformation of his world, including himself, and the consequent loss of the dimension of depth in his encounter with reality. Reality has lost its inner transcendence or, in another metaphor, its transparency for the eternal. The system of finite interrelations which we call the universe has become self-sufficient. It is calculable and manageable and can be improved from the point of view of man's needs and desires. Since the beginning of the 18th century God has been removed from the power field of man's activities. He has been put alongside the world without permission to interfere with it because every interference would disturb man's technical and business calculations. The result is that God has become superfluous and the universe left to man as its master. This situation leads to the second characteristic of industrial society.

In order to fulfill his destiny, man must be in possession of creative powers, analogous to those previously attributed to God, and so creativity must become a human quality. The conflict between what man essentially is and what he actually is, his estrangement, or in traditional terms his fallen state, is disregarded. Death and guilt disappear even in the preaching of early industrial society. Their acknowledgment would interfere with man's progressive conquest of nature, outside and inside himself. Man has shortcomings, but there is no sin and certainly no universal sinfulness. The bondage of the will, of which the Reformer spoke, the demonic powers which are central for the New Testament, the structures of destruction in personal and communal life, are ignored or denied. Educational processes are able to adjust the large majority of men to the demands of the system of production and consumption. Man's actual state is hence mistakenly regarded as his essential state, and he is pictured in a position of progressive fulfillment of his potentialities.

This is supposed to be true not only of man as an individual personality, but also of man as community. The scientific and technical conquest of time and space is considered as the road to the reunion of mankind. The demonic structures of history, the conflicts of power in every realization of life are seen as preliminary impediments. Their tragic and inescapable character is denied. As the universe replaces God, as man in the center of the universe replaces the Christ, so the expectation of peace and justice in history replaces the expectation of the Kingdom of God. The dimension of depth in the divine and demonic has disappeared. This is the spirit of industrial society manifest in the style of its creations.

The attitude of the churches toward this situation was contradictory. Partly they defended themselves by retiring to their traditional past in doctrine, cult, and life. But in so doing, they used the categories created by the industrial spirit against which they were fighting. They drew the symbols in which the depth of being expresses itself down to the level of ordinary, so to speak, two-dimensional experiences. They understood them literally and defended their validity by establishing a supranatural above the natural realm. But supranaturalism is only the counterpart of naturalism and vice versa. They produce each other in never-ending fights against each other. Neither could live without its opposite.

The impossibility of this kind of defense of the tradition was recognized by the other way in which the churches reacted to the spirit of industrial society. They accepted the new situation and tried to adapt themselves to it by reinterpreting the traditional symbols in contemporary terms. This is the justification and even the glory of what we call today "liberal theology." But it must also be stated that in its theological understanding of God and man, liberal theology paid the price of adjustment by losing the message of the new reality which was preserved by its supranaturalistic defenders. Both ways in which the churches dealt with the spirit of industrial society proved to be inadequate.

While naturalism and supranaturalism, liberalism and orthodoxy were involved in undecisive struggles, historical providence prepared another way of relating religion to contemporary culture. This preparation was done in the depth of industrial civilization, sometimes by people who represented it in its most anti-religious implications. This is the large movement known as existentialism which started with

Pascal, was carried on by a few prophetic minds in the 19th century and came to a full victory in the 20th century.

Existentialism, in the largest sense, is the protest against the spirit of industrial society within the framework of industrial society. The protest is directed against the position of man in the system of production and consumption of our society. Man is supposed to be the master of his world and of himself. But actually he has become a part of the reality he has created, an object among objects, a thing among things, a cog within a universal machine to which he must adapt himself in order not to be smashed by it. But this adaptation makes him a means for ends which are means themselves, and in which an ultimate end is lacking. Out of this predicament of man in the industrial society the experiences of emptiness and meaninglessness, of dehumanization and estrangement have resulted. Man has ceased to encounter reality as meaningful. Reality in its ordinary forms and structures does not speak to him any longer.

One way out is that man restricts himself to a limited section of reality and defends it against the intrusion of the world into his castle. This is the neurotic way out which becomes psychotic if reality disappears completely. It involves subjection to the demands of culture and repression of the question of meaning. Or some may have the strength to take anxiety and meaninglessness courageously upon themselves and live creatively, expressing the predicament of the most sensitive people in our time in cultural production. It is the latter way to which we owe the artistic and philosophical works of culture in the first half of the 20th century. They are creative expressions of the destructive trends in contemporary culture. The great works of the visual arts, of music, of poetry, of literature, of architecture, of dance, of philosophy, show in their style both the encounter with non-being, and the strength which can stand this encounter and shape it creatively. Without this key, contemporary culture is a closed door. With this key, it can be understood as the revelation of man's predicament, both in the present world and in the world universally. This makes the protesting element in contemporary culture theologically significant.

THE CULTURAL FORMS IN WHICH RELIGION ACTUALIZES ITSELF

The form of religion is culture. This is especially obvious in the language used by religion. Every language, including that of the Bible, is the result of innumerable acts of cultural creativity. All functions of man's spiritual life are based on man's power to speak vocally or silently. Language is the expression of man's freedom from the given situation and its concrete demands. It gives him universals in whose power he can create worlds above the given world of technical civilization and spiritual content.

Conversely, the development of these worlds determines the development of language. There is no sacred language which has fallen from a supranatural heaven and been put between the covers of a book. But there is human language, based on man's encounter with reality, changing through the millenia, used for the needs of daily life, for expression and communication, for literature and poetry, and used also for the expression and communication of our ultimate concern. In each of these cases the language is different. Religious language is ordinary language, changed under the power of what it expresses, the ultimate of being and meaning. The expression of it can be narrative (mythological, legendary, historical), or it can be prophetic, poetic, liturgical. It becomes holy for those to whom it expresses their ultimate concern from generation to generation. But there is no holy language in itself, as translations, retranslations and revisions show.

This leads to a second example of the use of cultural creations within religion: religious art. One principle which must be emphasized again and again in religious art is the principle of artistic honesty. There is no sacred artistic style in Protestant, in contrast, for example, to Greek-Orthodox doctrine. An artistic style is honest only if it expresses the real situation of the artist and the cultural period to which he belongs. We can participate in the artistic styles of the past in so far as they were honestly expressing the encounter which they had with God, man, and world. But we cannot honestly imitate them and produce for the cult of the Church works which are not the result of a creating ecstasy, but which are learned reproductions of creative ecstasies of the past. It was a religiously significant achievement of modern architecture that it liberated itself from traditional forms which, in the context of our period, were nothing but trimmings without meaning and, therefore, neither aesthetically valuable nor religiously expressive.

A third example is taken from the cognitive realm. It is the question: what elements of the contemporary philosophical consciousness can be used for the theological interpretation of the Christian symbols? If we take the existentialist protest against the spirit of industrial society seriously, we must reject both naturalism and idealism as tools for theological self-expression. Both of them are creations of that spirit against which the protest of our century is directed. Both of them have been used by theology in sharply conflicting methods, but neither of them expresses the contemporary culture.

Instead, theology must use the immense and profound material of the existential analysis in all cultural realms, including therapeutic psychology. But theology cannot use it by simply accepting it. Theology must confront it with the answer implied in the Christian message. The confrontation of the existential analysis with the symbol in which Christianity has expressed its ultimate concern is the method which is adequate both to the message of Jesus as the Christ and to the human predicament as rediscovered in contemporary culture. The answer cannot be derived from the question. It is said *to* him who asks, but it is not taken *from* him. Existentialism cannot give answers. It can determine the form of the answer, but whenever an existentialist artist or philosopher answers, he does so through the power of another tradition which has revelatory sources. To give such answers is the function of the Church not only to itself, but also to those outside the Church.

THE INFLUENCES OF THE CHURCH ON CONTEMPORARY CULTURE

The Church has the function of answering the question implied in man's very existence, the question of the meaning of this existence. One of the ways in which the Church does this is evangelism. The principle of evangelism must be to show to the people outside the Church that the symbols in which the life of the Church expresses itself are answers to the questions implied in their very existence as human beings. Because the Christian message is the message of salvation and because salvation means healing, the message of healing in every sense of the word is appropriate to our situation. This is the reason why movements at the fringe of the Church, sectarian and evangelistic movements of a most primitive and unsound character, have such great success. Anxiety and despair about existence itself induces millions of people to look out for any kind of healing that promises success.

The Church cannot take this way. But it must understand that the average kind of preaching is unable to reach the people of our time. They must feel that Christianity is not a set of doctrinal or ritual or moral laws, but is rather the good news of the conquest of the law by the appearance of a new healing reality. They must feel that the Christian symbols are not absurdities, unacceptable for the questioning mind of our period, but that they point to that which alone is of ultimate concern, the ground and meaning of our existence and of existence generally.

There remains a last question, namely, the question of how the Church should deal with the spirit of our society which is responsible for much of what must be healed by the Christian message. Has the Church the task and the power to attack and to transform the spirit of industrial society? It certainly cannot try to replace the present social reality by another one, in terms of a progress to the realized Kingdom of God. It cannot sketch perfect social structures or suggest concrete reforms. Cultural changes occur by the inner dynamics of culture itself. The Church participates in them, sometimes in a leading role, but then it is a cultural force beside others and not the representative of the new reality in history.

In its prophetic role the Church is the guardian who reveals dynamic structures in society and undercuts their demonic power by revealing them, even within the Church itself. In so doing the Church listens to prophetic voices outside itself, judging both the culture and the Church in so far as it is a part of the culture. We have referred to such prophetic voices in our culture. Most of them are not active members of the manifest Church. But perhaps one could call them participants of a "latent Church," a Church in which the ultimate concern which drives the manifest Church is hidden under cultural forms and deformations.

Sometimes this latent Church comes into the open. Then the manifest Church should recognize in these voices what its own spirit should be and accept them even if they appear hostile to the Church. But the Church should also stand as a guardian against the demonic distortions into which attacks must fall if they are not grasped by the right subject of our ultimate concern. This was the fate of the communist movement. The Church was not sufficiently aware of its function as guardian when this movement was still undecided about its way. The Church did not hear the prophetic voice in communism and therefore did not recognize its demonic possibilities.

Judging means seeing both sides. The Church judges culture, including the Church's own forms of life. For its forms are created by culture, as its religious substance makes culture possible. The Church and culture are within, not alongside, each other. And the Kingdom of God includes both while transcending both.

II. CONCRETE APPLICATIONS

V

The Nature of Religious Language

THE fact that there is so much discussion about the meaning of symbols going on in this country as well as in Europe is a symptom of something deeper, something both negative and positive in its import. It is a symptom of the fact that we are in a confusion of language in theology and philosophy and related subjects which has hardly been surpassed at any time in history. Words do not communicate to us any more what they originally did and what they were invented to communicate. This has something to do with the fact that our present culture has no clearing house such as medieval scholasticism was, Protestant scholasticism in the 17th century at least tried to be, and philosophers like Kant tried to renew. We have no such clearing house, and this is the one point at which we might be in sympathy with the present day so-called logical positivists or symbolic logicians or logicians generally. They at least try to produce a clearing house. The only criticism is that this clearing house is a very small room, perhaps only a corner of a house, and not a real house. It excludes most of life. But it could become useful if it increased in reach and acceptance of realities beyond the mere logical calculus.

The positive point is that we are in a process in which a very important thing is being rediscovered: namely, that there are levels of reality of great difference, and that these different levels demand different approaches and different languages; not everything in reality can be grasped by the language which is most adequate for mathematical sciences. The insight into this situation is the most positive side of the fact that the problem of symbols is again taken seriously.

I.

Let us proceed with the intention of clearing concepts as much as we are able, and let us take five steps, the first of which is the discussion of "symbols and signs." Symbols are similar to signs in one decisive respect: both symbols and signs point beyond themselves to something else. The typical sign, for instance the red light at the corner of the street, does not point to itself but it points to the necessity of cars stopping. And every symbol points beyond itself to a reality for which it stands. In this, symbols and signs have an essential identity—they point beyond themselves. And this is the reason that the confusion of language mentioned above has also conquered the discussion about symbols for centuries and has produced confusion between signs and symbols. The first step in any clearing up of the meaning of symbols is to distinguish it from the meaning of signs.

The difference, which is a fundamental difference between them, is that signs do not participate in any way in the reality and power of that to which they point. Symbols, although they are not the same as that which they symbolize, participate in its meaning and power. The difference between symbol and sign is the participation in the symbolized reality which characterizes the symbols, and the non-participation in the "pointed-to" reality which characterizes a sign. For example, letters of the alphabet as they are written, an "A" or an "R" do not participate in the sound to which they point; on the other hand, the flag participates in the power of the king or the nation for which it stands and which it symbolizes. There has, therefore, been a fight since the days of William Tell as to how to behave in the presence of the flag. This would be meaningless if the flag did not participate as a symbol in the power of that which it symbolizes. The whole monarchic idea is itself entirely incomprehensible, if you do not understand that the king always is both: on the one hand, a symbol of the power of the group of which he is the king and on the other hand, he who exercises partly (never fully, of course) this power.

But something has happened which is very dangerous for all our attempts to find a clearing house for the concepts of symbols and signs. The mathematician has usurped the term "symbol" for mathematical "sign," and this makes a disentanglement of the confusion almost impossible. The only thing we can do is to distinguish different groups, signs which are called symbols, and genuine symbols. The mathematical signs are signs which are wrongly called symbols.

Language is a very good example of the difference between signs and symbols. Words in a language are signs for a meaning which they express. The word "desk" is a sign which points to something quite different—namely, the thing on which a paper is lying and at which we might be looking. This has nothing to do with the word "desk," with these four letters. But there are words in every language which are more than this, and in the moment in which they get connotations which go beyond something to which they point as signs, then they can become symbols; and this is a very important distinction for any speaker. He can speak almost completely in signs, reducing the meaning of his words almost to mathematical signs, and this is the absolute ideal of the logical positivist. The other pole of this is liturgical or poetic language where words have a power through centuries, or more than centuries. They have connotations in situations in which they appear so that they cannot be replaced. They have become not only signs pointing to a meaning which is defined, but also symbols standing for a reality in the power of which they participate.

II.

Now we come to a second consideration dealing with the functions of symbols. The first function is implied in what has already been said—namely, the representative function. The symbol represents something which is not itself, for which it stands and in the power and meaning of which it participates. This is a basic function of every symbol, and therefore, if that word had not been used in so many other ways, one could perhaps even translate "symbolic" as "representative," but for some reason that is not possible. If the symbols stand for something which they are not, then the question is, "Why do we not have that for which they stand directly? Why do we need symbols at all?" And now we come to something which is perhaps the main function of the symbol—namely, the opening up of levels of reality which otherwise are hidden and cannot be grasped in any other way.

Every symbol opens up a level of reality for which nonsymbolic speaking is inadequate. Let us interpret this, or explain this, in terms of artistic symbols. The more we try to enter into the meaning of symbols, the more we become aware that it is a function of art to open up levels of reality;

in poetry, in visual art, and in music, levels of reality are opened up which can be opened up in no other way. Now if this is the function of art, then certainly artistic creations have symbolic character. You can take that which a landscape of Rubens, for instance, mediates to you. You cannot have this experience in any other way than through this painting made by Rubens. This landscape has some heroic character; it has character of balance, of colors, of weights, of values, and so on. All this is very external. What this mediates to you cannot be expressed in any other way than through the painting itself. The same is true also in the relationship of poetry and philosophy. The temptation may often be to confuse the issue by bringing too many philosophical concepts into a poem. Now this is really the problem; one cannot do this. If one uses philosophical language or scientific language, it does not mediate the same thing which is mediated in the use of really poetic language without a mixture of any other language.

This example may show what is meant by the phrase "opening up of levels of reality." But in order to do this, something else must be opened up—namely, levels of the soul, levels of our interior reality. And they must correspond to the levels in exterior reality which are opened up by a symbol. So every symbol is two-edged. It opens up reality and it opens up the soul. There are, of course, people who are not opened up by music or who are not opened up by poetry, or more of them (especially in Protestant America) who are not opened up at all by visual arts. The "opening up" is a two-sided function—namely, reality in deeper levels and the human soul in special levels.

If this is the function of symbols then it is obvious that symbols cannot be replaced by other symbols. Every symbol has a special function which is just *it* and cannot be replaced by more or less adequate symbols. This is different from signs, for signs can always be replaced. If one finds that a green light is not so expedient as perhaps a blue light (this is not true, but could be true), then we simply put on a blue light, and nothing is changed. But a symbolic word (such as the word "God") cannot be replaced. No symbol can be replaced when used in its special function. So one asks rightly, "How do symbols arise, and how do they come to an end?" As different from signs, symbols are born and die. Signs are consciously invented and removed. This is a fundamental difference.

"Out of what womb are symbols born?" Out of the womb which is usually called today the "group unconscious" or "collective unconscious," or whatever you want to call it— out of a group which acknowledges, in this thing, this word, this flag, or whatever it may be, its own being. It is not invented intentionally; and even if somebody would try to invent a symbol, as sometimes happens, then it becomes a symbol only if the unconscious of a group says "yes" to it. It means that something is opened up by it in the sense which I have just described. Now this implies further that in the moment in which this inner situation of the human group to a symbol has ceased to exist, then the symbol dies. The symbol does not "say" anything any more. In this way, all of the polytheistic gods have died; the situation in which they were born, has changed or does not exist any more, and so the symbols died. But these are events which cannot be described in terms of intention and invention.

III.

Now we come to a third consideration—namely, the nature of religious symbols. Religious symbols do exactly the same thing as all symbols do—namely, they open up a level of reality, which otherwise is not opened at all, which is hidden. We can call this the depth dimension of reality itself, the dimension of reality which is the ground of every other dimension and every other depth, and which therefore, is not one level beside the others but is the fundamental level, the level below all other levels, the level of being itself, or the ultimate power of being. Religious symbols open up the experience of the dimension of this depth in the human soul. If a religious symbol has ceased to have this function, then it dies. And if new symbols are born, they are born out of a changed relationship to the ultimate ground of being, i.e., to the Holy.

The dimension of ultimate reality is the dimension of the Holy. And so we can also say, religious symbols are symbols of the Holy. As such they participate in the holiness of the Holy according to our basic definition of a symbol. But participation is not identity; they are not themselves *the* Holy. The wholly transcendent transcends every symbol of the Holy. Religious symbols are taken from the infinity of material which the experienced reality gives us. Everything in time and space has become at some time in the history of religion a symbol for the Holy. And this is naturally so, because everything that is in the world we encounter rests on the ultimate ground of being. This is the key to the otherwise extremely confusing history of religion. Those of you who have looked into this seeming chaos of the history of religion in all periods of history from the earliest primitives to the latest developments, will be extremely confused about the chaotic character of this development. The key which makes order out of this chaos is comparatively simple. It is that everything in reality can impress itself as a symbol for a special relationship of the human mind to its own ultimate ground and meaning. So in order to open up the seemingly closed door to this chaos of religious symbols, one simply has to ask, "What is the relationship to the ultimate which is symbolized in these symbols?" And then they cease to be meaningless; and they become, on the contrary, the most revealing creations of the human mind, the most genuine ones, the most powerful ones, those who control the human consciousness, and perhaps even more the unconsciousness, and have therefore this tremendous tenacity which is characteristic of all religious symbols in the history of religion.

Religion, as everything in life, stands under the law of ambiguity, "ambiguity" meaning that it is creative and destructive at the same time. Religion has its holiness and its unholiness, and the reason for this is obvious from what has been said about religious symbolism. Religious symbols point symbolically to that which transcends all of them. But since, as symbols, they participate in that to which they point, they always have the tendency (in the human mind, of course) to replace that to which they are supposed to point, and to become ultimate in themselves. And in the moment in which they do this, they become idols. All idolatry is nothing else than the absolutizing of symbols of the Holy, and making them identical with the Holy itself. In this way, for instance, holy persons can become a god. Ritual acts can take on unconditional validity, although they are only expressions of a special situation. In all sacramental activities of religion, in all holy objects, holy books, holy doctrines, holy rites, you find this danger which we will call "demonization." They become demonic at the moment in which they become elevated to the unconditional and ultimate character of the Holy itself.

IV.

Now we turn to a fourth consideration—namely, the levels of religious symbols. There are two fundamental levels in all religious symbols: the transcendent level, the level which goes *beyond* the empirical reality we encounter, and the immanent level, the level which we find *within* the encounter with reality. Let us look at the first level, the transcendent level. The basic symbol on the transcendent level would be God himself. But we cannot simply say that God is a symbol. We must always say two things about him: we must say that there is a non-symbolic element in our image of God—namely, that he is ultimate reality, being itself, ground of being, power of being; and the other, that he is the highest being in which everything that we have does exist in the most perfect way. If we say this we have in our mind the image of a highest being, a being with the characteristics of highest perfection. That means we have a symbol for that which is not symbolic in the idea of God—namely, "Being Itself."

It is important to distinguish these two elements in the idea of God. Thus all of these discussions going on about God being a person or not a person, God being similar to other beings or not similar, these discussions which have a great impact on the destruction of the religious experience through false interpretations of it, could be overcome if we would say, "Certainly the awareness of something unconditional is in itself what it is, is not symbolic." We can call it *"Being Itself,"* *esse qua esse, esse ipsum,* as the scholastics did. But in our relationship to this ultimate we symbolize and must symbolize. We could not be in communication with God if he were only "ultimate being." But in our relationship to him we encounter him with the highest of what we ourselves are, *person.* And so in the symbolic form of speaking about him, we have both that which transcends infinitely our experience of ourselves as persons, and that which is so adequate to our being persons that we can say, "Thou" to God, and can pray to him. And these two elements must be preserved. If we preserve only the element of the unconditional, then no relationship to God is possible. If we preserve only the element of the ego-thou relationship, as it is called today, we lose the element of the divine—namely, the unconditional which transcends subject and object and all other polarities. This is the first point on the transcendent level.

The second is the qualities, the attributes of God, whatever you say about him: that he is love, that he is mercy, that he is power, that he is omniscient, that he is omnipresent, that he is almighty. These attributes of God are taken from experienced qualities we have ourselves. They cannot be applied to God in the literal sense. If this is done, it leads to an infinite amount of absurdities. This again is one of the reasons for the destruction of religion through wrong communicative interpretation of it. And again the symbolic character of these qualities must be maintained consistently. Otherwise, every speaking about the divine becomes absurd.

A third element on the transcendent level is the acts of God, for example, when we say, "He has created the world," "He has sent his son," "He will fulfill the world." In all these temporal, causal, and other expressions we speak symbolically of God. As an example, look at the one small sentence: "*God has sent his son.*" Here we have in the word "has" temporality. But God is beyond *our* temporality, though not beyond every temporality. Here is space; "sending somebody" means moving him from one place to another place. This certainly is speaking symbolically, although spatiality is in God as an element in his creative ground. We say that he "has sent"— that means that he has caused something. In this way God is subject to the category of causality. And when we speak of him and his Son, we have two different substances and apply the category of substance to him. Now all this, if taken literally, is absurd. If it is taken symbolically, it is a profound expression, the ultimate Christian expression, of the relationship between God and man in the Christian experience. But to distinguish these two kinds of speech, the non-symbolic and the symbolic, in such a point is so important that if we are not able to make understandable to our contemporaries that we speak symbolically when we use such language, they will rightly turn away from us, as from people who still live in absurdities and superstitions.

Now consider the immanent level, the level of the appearances of the divine in time and space. Here we have first of all the incarnations of the divine, different beings in time and space, divine beings transmuted into animals or men or any kinds of other beings as they appear in time and space. This is often forgotten by those within Christianity who like to use in every second theological proposition the word "incarnation." They forget that this is not an especially Christian characteristic, because incarnation is something which happens in paganism all the time. The divine beings always incarnate in different forms. That is very easy in paganism. This is not the real distinction between Christianity and other religions.

Here we must say something about the relationships of the transcendent to the immanent level just in connection with the incarnation idea. Historically, one must say that preceding both of them was the situation in which the transcendent and immanent were not distinguished. In the Indonesian doctrine of "Mana," that divine mystical power which permeates all reality, we have some divine presence which is both immanent in everything as a hidden power, and at the same time transcendent, something which can be grasped only through very difficult ritual activities known to the priest.

Out of this identity of the immanent and the transcendent, the gods of the great mythologies have developed in Greece and in the Semitic nations and in India. There we find incarnations as the immanent element of the divine. The more transcendent the gods become, the more incarnations of personal or sacramental character are needed in order to overcome the remoteness of the divine which develops with the strengthening of the transcendent element.

And from this follows the second element in the immanent religious symbolism, namely, the sacramental. The sacramental is nothing else than some reality becoming the bearer of the Holy in a special way and under special circumstances. In this sense, the Lord's Supper, or better the materials in the Lord's Supper, are symbolic. Now you will ask perhaps, "only symbolic?" That sounds as if there were something more than symbolic, namely, "literal." But the literal is not more but less than symbolic. If we speak of those dimensions of reality which we cannot approach in any other way than by symbols, then symbols are not used in terms of "only" but in terms of that which is necessary, of that which we *must* apply. Sometimes, because of nothing more than the confusion of signs with symbols, the phrase "only a symbol" means "only a sign." And then the question is justified. "Only a sign?" "No." The sacrament is not only a sign. In the famous discussion between Luther and Zwingli, in Marburg in 1529, it was just this point on which the discussion was held. Luther wanted to maintain the genuinely symbolic character of the elements, but Zwingli said that the sacramental materials, bread and wine, are "only symbolic." Thus Zwingli meant that they are only signs pointing to a story of the past. Even in that period there was semantic confusion. And let us not be mislead by this. In the real sense of symbol, the sacramental materials are symbols. But if the symbol is used as *only* symbol (i.e., only signs), then of course the sacramental materials are more than this.

Then there is the third element on the immanent level. Many things—like special parts of the church building, like the candles, like the water at the entrance of the Roman Church, like the cross in all churches, especially Protestant churches—were originally only signs, but in use became symbols; call them sign-symbols, signs which have become symbols.

V.

And now a last consideration—namely, the truth of religious symbols. Here we must distinguish a negative, a positive, and an absolute statement. First the negative statement. Symbols are independent of any empirical criticism. You cannot kill a symbol by criticism in terms of natural sciences or in terms of historical research. As was said, symbols can only die if the situation in which they have been created has passed. They are not on a level on which empirical criticism can dismiss them. Here are two examples, both connected with Mary, the mother of Jesus, as Holy Virgin. First of all you have here a symbol which has died in Protestantism by the changed situation of the relation to God. The special, direct, immediate relationship to God, makes any mediating power impossible. Another reason which has made this symbol disappear is the negation of the ascetic element which is implied in the glorification of virginity. And as long as the Protestant religious situation lasts it cannot be re-established. It has not died because Protestant scholars have said, "Now there is no empirical reason for saying all this about the Holy Virgin." There certainly is not, but this the Roman Church also knows. But the Roman Church sticks to it on the basis of its tremendous symbolic power which step by step brings her nearer to Trinity itself, especially in the development of the last decade. If this should ever be completed as is now discussed in groups of the Roman Church, Mary would become co-Saviour with Jesus. Then, whether this is admitted or not, she is actually taken into the divinity itself.

Another example is the story of the virginal birth of Jesus. This is from the point of view of historical research a most obviously legendary story, unknown to Paul and to John. It is a late creation, trying to make understandable the full possession of the divine Spirit of Jesus of Nazareth. But again its legendary character is not the reason why this symbol will die or has died in many groups of people, in even quite conservative groups within the Protestant churches. The reason is different. The reason is that it is theologically quasi-heretical. It takes away one of the fundamental doctrines of Chalcedon, viz., the classical Christian doctrine that the full humanity of Jesus must be maintained beside his whole divinity. A human being who has no human father has no full humanity. This story then has to be criticized on inner-symbolic grounds, but not on historical grounds. This is the negative statement about the truth of religious symbols. Their truth is their adequacy to the religious situation in which they are created, and their inadequacy to another situation is their untruth. In the last sentence both the postive and the negative statement about symbols are contained.

Religion is ambiguous and every religious symbol may become idolatrous, may be demonized, may elevate itself to ultimate validity although nothing is ultimate but the ultimate itself; no religious doctrine and no religious ritual may be. If Christianity claims to have a truth superior to any other truth in its symbolism, then it is the symbol of the cross in which this is expressed, the cross of the Christ. He who himself embodies the fullness of the divine's presence sacrifices himself in order not to become an idol, another god beside God, a god into whom the disciples wanted to make him. And therefore the decisive story is the story in which he accepts the title "Christ" when Peter offers it to him. He accepts it under the one condition that he has to go to Jerusalem to suffer and to die, which means to deny the idolatrous tendency even with respect to himself. This is at the same time the criterion of all other symbols, and it is the criterion to which every Christian church should subject itself.

VI

Protestantism and Artistic Style

PICASSO's "Guernica" is a great Protestant painting. Of course, this statement must be qualified by saying that it is not the Protestant answer, but rather the radicalism of the Protestant question which one can find in Picasso's masterpiece. It is to this assertion that the following chapter is directed.

First, something must be said about the particular character of the Protestant understanding of man and his predicament. The Protestant principle (which is not always effective in the preaching and teaching of the Protestant churches) emphasizes the infinite distance between God and man. It emphasizes man's finitude, his subjection to death, but above all, his estrangement from his true being and his bondage to demonic forces—forces of self-destruction. Man's inability to liberate himself from this bondage has led the Reformers to the doctrine of a reunion with God in which God alone acts and man only receives. Such receiving, of course, is not possible in an attitude of passivity, but it demands the highest courage, namely the courage to accept the paradox that "the sinner is justified," that it is man in anxiety, guilt, and despair who is the object of God's unconditional acceptance.

If we consider Picasso's "Guernica" as an example—perhaps *the* outstanding one—of an artistic expression of the human predicament in our period, its negative-Protestant character is obvious. The question of man in a world of guilt, anxiety, and despair is put before us with tremendous power. But it is not the subject matter—the willful and brutal destruction of a small town by Fascist airplanes—which gives the picture its expressive force; rather, it is its style. In spite of profound differences between the individual artists and between the different periods in the development of Picasso himself, this style is characteristic for the twentieth century and, in this sense, it is contemporaneous with us. A comparison of any important creation within this period with equally important creations of any earlier period shows the stylistic unity of the visual arts in the twentieth century. And this style, as no other one during the history of Protestantism, is able to express the human situation as Christianity sees it.

In order to verify this assertion, it is necessary to discuss the relation of artistic styles to religion generally. Every work of art shows three elements: subject matter, form, style. The subject matter is potentially identical with everything which can be received by the human mind in sensory images. It is in no way limited by other qualities like good or bad, beautiful or ugly, whole or broken, human or inhuman, divine or demonic. But not every subject matter is used by every artist or artistic period. There are principles of selection dependent on form and style, the second and third elements of a work of art.

The second element is a concept which is not an ordinary one. It belongs to the structural elements of being itself and can be understood only as that which makes a thing what it is. It gives a thing its uniqueness and universality, its special place within the whole of being, its expressive power. Artistic creation is determined by the form which uses particular materials such as sounds, words, stones, colors and elevates them to a work which stands on its own. For this reason, the form is the ontologically decisive element in every artistic creation—as in any other creation. But the form itself is qualified by the third element which we call style. This term, first used to describe changing fashions in clothing, houses, gardens, etc., has been applied to the realm of artistic production universally and has even been used in relation to philosophy, politics, etc. The style qualifies the many creations of a period in a unique way. It is due to their form that they are creations. It is due to their style that they have something in common.

The problem of style is one of finding what it is that these creations of the same style have in common. To what do they all point? Deriving my answer from many analyses of style, both in art and philosophy, I would say that every style points to a self-interpretation of man, thus answering the question of the ultimate meaning of life. Whatever the subject matter which an artist chooses, however strong or weak his artistic form, he cannot help but betray by his style his own ultimate concern, as well as that of his group, and his period. He cannot escape religion even if he rejects religion, for religion is the state of being ultimately concerned. And in every style the ultimate concern of a human group or period is manifest. It is one of the most fascinating tasks to decipher the religious meaning of styles of the past such as the archaic, the classic, the naturalistic, and to discover that the same characteristics which one discovered in an artistic creation can also be found in the literature, philosophy, and morals of a period.

The deciphering of a style is an art in itself and, like every art, is a matter of daring and risk. Styles have been contrasted with each other in several respects. If one looks at the series of styles in the visual arts in Western history after the beginnings of a Christian art in catacombs and basilicas, one is overwhelmed by its richness and variety: the Byzantine, the

Romanesque, the early and late Gothic styles precede the Renaissance in which the early and the high Renaissance styles must be distinguished. Mannerism, Baroque, Rococo, Classicism, Romanticism, Naturalism, Impressionism, Expressionism, Cubism, Surrealism lead to the contemporary non-representative style. Each of them says something about the period in which they were flourishing. In each of them a self-interpretation of man is indicated, although in most cases the artists were not aware of such interpretation. Sometimes they knew what they expressed. And sometimes philosophers and art critics made them aware of it. What then are the keys which aid in deciphering the meaning of these styles?

In a famous analysis of philosophical styles, the German philosopher, Dilthey, distinguished subjective idealism, objective idealism, and realism. In this way he gave four stylistic keys which can immediately be applied to the visual arts: idealistic, realistic, subjective, objective. Every work of art contains elements of all four, but is under the predominance of one or more of them. When in the beginning of this century the predominance of the classicist style was broken and the aesthetic value of the Gothic style became visible, other keys were discovered. With the rise of Expressionism the fundamental contrast of the imitating and the expressive element became decisive for the analysis of many past and present styles, especially for the understanding of primitive art. Further, one can distinguish monumental and idyllic, particularizing and abstracting, organic and inorganic stylistic elements. Finally, one can point to the continuous struggle between academic and revolutionary tendencies in artistic creation.

It would be a useless schematization if one tried to arrange these elements into an embracing system. But one thing must be said about all of them: They are never completely absent in any particular work of art. This is impossible because the structure of a work of art as a work of art demands the presence of all elements which provide the keys for the deciphering of a style. Since a work of art is the work of an artist, the subjective element is always present. Since he uses materials found in ordinarily encountered reality, the imitating element is unavoidable. Since he comes from a tradition and cannot escape it even if he revolts against it, an academic element is always present. Since he transforms reality by the very fact that he creates a work of art, an idealistic element is effective. And if he wants to express an original encounter with reality below its surface, he uses expressive elements. But in the process of artistic creativity some elements are suppressed to a point where it is difficult to recognize them. This difficulty usually results from a combination of stylistic elements, and makes the analysis of styles fruitful and fascinating.

We must now ask the question: What is the relation of these style-determining elements to religion generally and especially to Protestantism? Are certain styles more able to express religious subject matter than others? Are certain styles essentially religious and others essentially secular? The first answer must be that there is no style which excludes the artistic expression of man's ultimate concern, for the ultimate is not bound to any special form of things or experiences. It is present and may be absent in any situation. But the ways in which it is present are manifold. It can be present indirectly as the hidden ground of a situation. It shines through a landscape or a portrait or a human scene and gives them the depth of meaning. In this way a style in which the imitating element is predominant is religious in substance. The ultimate is present in experiences in which not only the reality is experienced, but the encounter itself with reality. It is hiddenly present in the state of being grasped by the power of being and meaning in reality. This gives religious significance to the stylistic element of subjectivity and to styles in which it is predominant. And the ultimate is present in those encounters with reality in which the potential perfection of reality is anticipated and artistically expressed. This shows that a style in which the idealistic element is predominant is religious in substance. The ultimate is also present in those experiences of reality in which its negative, ugly, and self-destructive side is encountered. It is present as the divine-demonic and judging background of everything that is. This gives the realistic element in artistic styles its religious significance.

These examples could be increased by pointing to the religious significance of the other elements in artistic styles. But instead of doing so, let us look at the expressive element in a style, for it has a special relation to religion.

First, it must be said generally that there are definite adequacies and inadequacies between style and subject matter. This has the consequence that the preferred material varies with the predominance of one stylistic element or a combination of them, and it gives importance to iconography for the analysis of the meaning of styles. For example, one must look for the adequacy of special stylistic elements in portraits still-lifes, landscapes, human scenes, nude bodies, historical events, etc. We must restrict ourselves to the affinity of the expressive style to religion. It shares the general religious significance of all stylistic elements. But while the others are only indirectly representing the ultimate, the expressive element represents it directly. Of course, it usually does not appear alone in a work of art, and other elements may counterbalance its directly religious potentialities. But in itself it is essentially adequate to express religious meaning directly, both through the medium of secular and through the medium of traditional religious subject matter.

The reason for this situation is easy to find. The expressive element in a style implies a radical transformation of the ordinarily encountered reality by using elements of it in a way which does not exist in the ordinarily encountered reality. Expression disrupts the naturally given appearance of things. Certainly, they are united in the artistic form, but not in a way which the imitating or the idealistic or even the realistic element would demand. On the other hand, that which is expressed is not the subjectivity of the artist in the sense of the subjective element which is predominant in Impressionism and Romanticism. That which is expressed is the "dimension of depth" in the encountered reality, the ground and abyss in which everything is rooted.

This explains two important facts: the dominance of the expressive element in the style of all periods in which great religious art has been created and the directly religious effect of a style which is under the predominance of the expressive element, even if no material from any of the religious traditions is used. If this situation is compared with those periods in which the expressive element was prevented from becoming effective, one finds a definite difference. In styles which were under the control of non-expressive elements, the religious art deteriorated (as for instance in the last period of Western history) and the secular subject matter was hiding its religious background up to the point at which it became unrecognizable. Therefore, the rediscovery of the expressive element in art since about 1900 is a decisive event for the relation of religion and the visual arts. It has made religious art again possible.

This does not mean that we already have a great religious art. We do not have it either in terms of general religious art nor in terms of artistic creations suitable for devotional purposes. An exception to this judgment is recent church architecture in which a new beginning has been made permitting high expectations for future development. Architecture is the basic artistic expression, just because it is not only art but because it serves a practical purpose. It is quite probable that the renewal of religious art will start in co-operation with architecture.

If we look at painting and sculpture, we find that under the predominance of the expressive style in the last fifty years, the attempts to re-create religious art have led mostly to a rediscovery of the symbols in which the negativity of man's predicament is expressed: The symbol of the Cross has become the subject matter of many works of art—often in the style which is represented by Picasso's "Guernica." Symbols, such as resurrection, have not yet found any adequate artistic representation, and so it is with the other traditional "symbols of glory." This is the Protestant element in the present situation: No premature solutions should be tried; rather, the human situation in its conflicts should be expressed courageously. If it is expressed, it is already transcended: He who can bear and express guilt shows that he already knows about "acceptance-in-spite-of." He who can bear and express meaninglessness shows that he experiences meaning within his desert of meaninglessness.

The predominance of the expressive style in contemporary art is a chance for the rebirth of religious art. Not each of the varieties of this style is equally adequate to express religious symbols. But most of them definitely are. Whether, and to what degree, the artists (and the churches) will use this opportunity cannot be anticipated. It is partly dependent on the destiny of the traditional religious symbols themselves in their development during the next decades. The only thing we can do is to keep ourselves open for a new rise of religious art through the expressive style in the art of today.

VII

Existential Philosophy:

Its Historical Meaning

THE distinctive way of philosophizing which today calls itself *Existenzphilosophie* or "Existential philosophy" emerged
as one of the major currents of German thought under the
Weimar Republic, counting among its leaders such men as
Heidegger and Jaspers. But its history goes back at least a century, to the decade of the 1840's, when its main contentions
were formulated by thinkers like Schelling, Kierkegaard, and
Marx, in sharp criticism of the reigning "rationalism" or pan-
logism of the Hegelians; and in the next generation Nietzsche
and Dilthey were among its protagonists. Its roots are still
more ancient, deeply embedded in the pre-Cartesian German
tradition of supra-rationalism and *Innerlichkeit* represented
by Böhme.

Existential philosophy thus seems a specifically German
creation. It sprang originally from the tensions of the German
intellectual situation in the early nineteenth century. It has
been strongly influenced by the political and spiritual catas-
trophes of the Germans in our own generation. Its terminology
has been largely determined by the genius and often by the
demon of the German language—a fact which makes the
translation of Heidegger's *Sein und Zeit* so difficult.

But when we come to understand the import of the name

and the basic critical drive of Existential philosophy, we realize that it is part of a more general philosophical movement which counts its representatives in France, England, and America as well as in Germany. For in calling men back to "existence," these German thinkers are criticizing the identification of Reality or Being with Reality-as-known, with the object of Reason or thought.

Starting from the traditional distinction between "essence" and "existence," they insist that Reality or Being in its concreteness and fullness is not "essence." It is not the object of cognitive experience, but rather "existence" is Reality as immediately experienced, with the accent on the inner and personal character of man's immediate experience. Like Bergson, Bradley, James, and Dewey, the Existential philosophers are appealing from the conclusions of rationalistic thinking which equates Reality with the object of thought, with relations or "essence," to Reality as men experience it immediately in their actual living. They consequently take their place with all those who have regarded man's "immediate experience" as revealing more completely the nature and traits of Reality than man's cognitive experience. The philosophy of Existence is hence one version of that widespread appeal to immediate experience which has been so marked a feature of recent thought. In its influence not only on ideas but also on historical events, the international character of the movement is obvious—as witness the names of Marx, Nietzsche, and Bergson.

This appeal to "Existence" emerged just a hundred years ago in the decade from 1840 to 1850. During the winter of 1841–42 Schelling delivered his lectures on *Die Philosophie der Mythologie und der Offenbarung* in the University of Berlin before a distinguished audience including Engels, Kierkegaard, Bakunin, and Burckhardt. In 1840 Trendelenburg's *Logische Untersuchungen* had appeared. In 1843 Ludwig Feuerbach's *Grundsätze der Philosophie der Zukunft* came out. In 1844 Marx wrote his manuscript *National-ökonomie und Philosophie*, not published until a few years ago. The same year brought Max Stirner's *Der Einzige und sein Eigentum* and Kierkegaard's *Philosophical Fragments;* it also brought the second edition of Schopenhauer's *The World as Will and Idea*, which subsequently came to have a tremendous influence on Existential philosophy. In 1845–46 Marx wrote the manuscript of *Die Deutsche Ideologie*, including the *Thesen über Feuerbach*, and in 1846 Kierkegaard brought out the classic work of Existential philosophy, in the narrower sense of the term, *Concluding Unscientific Postscript.* Schelling's Berlin lectures are based on his development of the position achieved in the *Philosophy of Freedom* in 1809, and the *Weltalter* in 1811.[1] In his Munich lectures in the later twenties he had tried to show that the "postive philosophy," as he calls his type of Existential philosophy, had predecessors in men like Pascal, Jacobi, and Hamann, and in the theosophic tradition stemming from Böhme. Kant contributed to it through his Copernican revolution. Even in Plato "Existential" elements are obvious, especially in the non-dialectical method of the *Timaeus.* For Schelling takes the problem of the "positive philosophy" to be as old as philosophy itself. And in this Kierkegaard and Heidegger fully agree, as appears in Kierkegaard's use of the authority of Socrates, in Heidegger's close relation to Aristotle and Kant, and in the praise Lessing receives from all the Existential philosophers.

After this striking emergence of Existential philosophy in the fifth decade of the nineteenth century, the impulse of the

[1] The introduction to Schelling, *The Ages of the World*, translated with introduction and notes by Frederick de Wolfe Bolman, Jr. (New York, 1942), gives an excellent description of Schelling's development from an Essential to an Existential philosophy.

movement subsided; it was replaced by Neo-Kantian idealism or naturalistic empiricism. Feuerbach and Marx were interpreted as dogmatic materialists, Kierkegaard remained completely unknown, and Schelling's latest period was buried with a few contemptuous sentences in the textbooks on the history of philosophy. But a new impulse to "Existential" thinking came from the "*Lebensphilosophie*" or "Philosophy of Life" of the eighteen-eighties. During this decade Nietzsche's most important works appeared. In 1883 Dilthey published his *Einleitung in die Geisteswissenschaften*, and Bergson's *Essai sur les données immédiates de la conscience* came out in 1889. The "Philosophy of Life" is not identical with Existential philosophy. But if we understand the latter in a larger sense—as for historical and systematic reasons we must —then the "Philosophy of Life" includes most of the distinctive motives of Existential philosophy. Accordingly, we should also assign certain features of pragmatism, especially of William James's thought, to this philosophy of Existence as immediately experienced.

The third and contemporary form of Existential philosophy has resulted from a combination of this "Philosophy of Life" with Husserl's shift of emphasis from existent objects to the mind that makes them its objects, and with the rediscovery of Kierkegaard and of the early developments of Marx. Heidegger,[2] Jaspers,[3] and the Existential interpretation of history found in German "Religious Socialism"[4] are the main representatives of this third period of the philosophy of experienced Existence.

[2] Martin Heidegger, *Sein und Zeit* (Halle, 1927); *Kant und das Problem der Metaphysik* (Bonn, 1929).

[3] Karl Jaspers, *Philosophie*, 3 vols. (Berlin, 1938; 1st ed., 1932); *Vernunft und Existenz* (Groningen, 1935).

[4] Paul Tillich, *The Interpretation of History* (New York, 1936).

It is not proposed to give here a history of Existential philosophy. This has been done in rather fragmentary and implicit fashion by Karl Löwith,[5] Herbert Marcuse,[6] and others of the younger generation who have felt the actual impact on their lives of the problems emphasized by Existential philosophy. But we shall offer a comparative study of those ideas which are characteristic of most of the Existential philosophers, disregarding the distinctive features of their individual systems. The evaluation and interpretation of the significance of these ideas will remain implicit in the exposition and shall be stated explicitly only in a short conclusion.

I. THE METHODOLOGICAL FOUNDATIONS OF THE EXISTENTIAL PHILOSOPHY

1. The distinction between *essentia* and *existentia* in the philosophical tradition

The philosophy of Existence derives its name and its way of formulating its critical opposition to rationalistic views of Reality from the traditional distinction between "essence" and "existence." "Existence"—which comes from *existere*, meaning "emerge"—designates its root meaning "being" within the totality of Being, in distinction from "not being." *Dasein*, a word which has received a pregnant meaning in Heidegger's *Sein und Zeit*, adds the concrete element of "being in a special place," being *da* or "there." The scholastic distinction between *essentia* and *existentia* was the first step toward

[5] Karl Löwith, *Von Hegel bis Nietzsche* (Zürich, 1941).

[6] Herbert Marcuse, *Reason and Revolution* (New York and Oxford, 1941). See also Werner Brock, *Contemporary German Philosophy* (Cambridge, 1935).

giving a more significant meaning to the word "existence." In that distinction, "essence" signifies the What, the τί ἐστιν or *quid est* of a thing; "existence" signifies the That, the ὅτι ἐστιν or *quod est. Essentia* thus designates what a thing is *known* to be, the non-temporal object of knowledge in a temporal and changing thing, the οὐσία of that thing which makes it possible. But whether a thing is real or not is not implied in its essence: we do not know whether there is such a thing by knowing its "essence" alone. This must be decided by an existential proposition.

The assertion of the scholastics that in God essence and existence are identical is the second step in the development of the meaning of "existence." The Unconditioned cannot be conditioned by a difference between its essence and its existence. In absolute Being there is no possibility which is not an actuality: it is pure actuality. In all finite beings, on the other hand, this difference is present; in them existence as something separated from essence is the mark of finitude.

The third step in the enrichment of the term "existence" came from the discussion of the ontological argument, from its criticism by Kant and its re-establishment in a changed and broadened form by Hegel. This discussion brought out the fundamental fallacy involved. The ontological argument relies on the sound principle of the identity of Being and thinking, which all thinking presupposes: this identity is the *"Unvordenkliche"* (that principle prior to which thought cannot take place, the *Prius* of all thinking), as Schelling called it. But the argument surreptitiously transforms this principle into a highest Being, for the existence or non-existence of which demonstrations can be advanced. Kant's criticism of this interpretation is valid, but it does not touch the principle itself. On the contrary, Kant himself, in a powerful passage, describes the *Unvordenklichkeit* of Being-as-such from the point of view of an imagined highest Being who asks himself: Whence do I come? Hegel not only re-establishes the ontological argument in a purified form, he extends the principle of the identity of Being and thought to the whole of Being in so far as it is the "self-actualization of the Absolute." In this way he tries to overcome the separation of existence from essence in finite beings: for him, the finite is infinite both in its essence *and* in its existence.

2. Hegel's doctrine of essence and existence

The post-Hegelian attack on Hegel's dialectical system is directed against his attempt to absorb the whole of reality, not only in its essential but also in its existential and especially in its historical aspect, into the dialectical movement of "pure thought." The logical expression of this attempt is found in statements like these concerning essence and existence: "Essence *necessarily* appears." It transforms itself into existence. Existence is the being of essence, and therefore existence can be called "essential being." Essence *is* existence, it is not distinguished from its existence.[7]

It is in the light of these definitions that certain familiar propositions of Hegel's *Philosophy of Right* must be understood. If existence is essential being, reason is real and reality is rational. And therefore: "It is the task of philosophy to understand what is; for what is, is Reason . . . If philosophy builds a world as it ought to be, such a world can indeed be realized, but only in imagination, a plastic material on which anything can be impressed."[8] The task of philosophy is not to sketch an ideal world; on the contrary, we must say: the

[7] Hegel, *Logik*, ed. Lasson, II, 103, 105.

[8] Hegel, *Philosophie des Rechts*, ed. Lasson, 14, 15.

task of philosophy is "the reconciliation with reality." In contrast to this statement, it can be said: the task of Existential philosophy was first of all to destroy this Hegelian "reconciliation," which was merely conceptual, and left existence itself unreconciled.

3. Dialectical and temporal movement

Trendelenburg's *Logische Untersuchungen* seems to have made an impression on the post-Hegelian philosophers very similar to that made by Husserl's *Logische Untersuchungen* on the post-Neo-Kantians. He expresses his criticism of the dialectical movement in Hegel's *Logic* as follows: "Out of pure Being, which is explicitly an abstraction, and of Nothing—also an explicit abstraction—Becoming cannot suddenly emerge, this concrete intuition which controls life and death."[9] Two things are required—and implicitly supposed by Hegel—in order to "think" movement: a thinking subject and an intuition of time and space. The principle of negation, moreover, the driving force of the dialectical process, cannot lead to anything new without presupposing the experience of the thinking subject and an intuition of time and space. It is motion that distinguishes the realm of existence from the realm of essence.

Kierkegaard, who occasionally refers to Trendelenburg, expresses his insight as to the difference between merely dialectical and real Becoming in a more vivid way: "Pure thought is a recent invention and a 'lunatic postulate.' The negation of a preceding synthesis requires time. But time cannot find a place in pure thought."[10]

[9] Trendelenburg, *Logische Untersuchungen* (Berlin, 1840), 25.
[10] Kierkegaard, *Concluding Unscientific Postscript* (tr. Lowrie, Princeton, 1941).

Schelling calls the claim of Hegel's rational system to embrace not only the real, the What, but also its reality, the That, a "deception." No "merely logical process is also a process of real becoming."[11] When Hegel uses phrases such as: "the Idea decides to become Nature," or, "Nature is the fall of the Idea," he is either describing a real, non-dialectical event, or his terminology is meaningless.

Marx attacks in similar fashion the Hegelian transition from logic to Nature. He calls it "the fantastically described transition from the abstract thinker to sense experience."[12] But his criticism is more fundamental. It is directed against Hegel's category of *"Aufheben"* (which means both negating and preserving in a higher synthesis). "Because thinking is taken to imply at the same time its 'opposite,' sensible existence, and since it therefore claims that its motion is a real and sensed action, it believes that the process of '*Aufheben*' in thought, which in fact leaves the object as it is, has actually overcome the object."[13] This confusion between dialectical negation, which removes nothing but merely labels things as having been *"aufgehoben,"* and real revolutionary "negation" through practical activity, is responsible for the reactionary character of Hegel's dialectical system—in spite of its principle of negation. It is obvious that this criticism strikes not only Hegel, but every rational theory of progressive evolution, idealistic as well as naturalistic, including the later so-called "scientific Marxism."

[11] Schelling, *Sämtliche Werke*, Cotta ed. (Stuttgart, 1856–61), II, 3, 65.

[12] Marx, *Der Historische Materialismus*, ed. Alfred Kröner (Leipzig, 1932), I, 343.

[13] *Ibid.*, 338.

4. Possibility and actuality

The impotence of the "philosophy of essence" to explain existence is manifest in the fact that reason can deal only with possibilities: *Essentia est possibilitas*. Schelling writes: "Reason reaches what can be or will be—but only as an idea, and therefore, in comparison with real Being, only as a possibility."[14] Kierkegaard may have learned this from Schelling; he writes: "Abstract thought can grasp reality only by destroying it, and this destruction of reality consists in transforming it into mere possibility."[15] This is especially true of history: we cannot know an historical reality until we have resolved it into a mere possibility. "The only reality to which an existing individual may have a relation that is more than merely cognitive is his own reality, the fact that he exists."[16] Only in the aesthetic attitude—in Kierkegaard's psychology, the attitude of detachment—can we be related to "essence," the realm of possibility. In the aesthetic attitude, which includes the merely cognitive, there are always many possibilities, and in it no "decision" is demanded; in the ethical attitude a personal decision must always be made.

There is a very interesting statement by Marx making exactly the same point. He notes that according to Hegel "my real human existence is my philosophical existence." Hence, if our existential being comes to perfect realization only in the medium of thought, my real natural "existence" is my existence as a philosopher of nature; my real religious "existence" is my existence as a philosopher of religion. But this is the negation of religion as well as of humanity. This criticism

---

[14] Schelling, *Werke*, ii, 3, 66.

[15] Kierkegaard, *Concluding Unscientific Postscript*, 279.

[16] *Ibid.*, 128.

touches not only Hegel but also those who are trying to dissolve human existence into a mere scientific "possibility."

5. The immediate and personal experience of Existence

Since Existence cannot be approached rationally—since it is "external" to all thought, as Feuerbach and Schelling emphasize—it must be approached empirically. Schelling discusses empiricism at great length. He is so much in sympathy with it that he declares he would prefer English empiricism to the dialectical system of Hegel. He wrote the often-quoted and misquoted sentence that the true philosophers among the English and French are their great scientists. On the other hand, he differentiates between the various forms of "empiricism." He denies what he calls "sense empiricism," but he accepts what he calls "*a priori* empiricism." Of the latter he says, "Rational philosophy is likewise empirical with respect to its material."[17] But its truth does not depend on any existence. "It would be true even if nothing existed."[18] For its object is the realm of intelligible relations—of the *Sachverhalte*, as Husserl later called it.

As distinguished from such an "*a priori* empiricism," the approach of Existential philosophy to "Existence" is completely *a posteriori*. We experience "Existence" in the same way we experience a person through his actions. We do not draw conclusions from observed effects to their causes, but we encounter a person immediately in his utterances. In the same way, Schelling suggests, we should look at the world-process as the continuous self-revelation of the *Unvordenk-*

[17] Schelling, *Werke*, II, 3, 102.

[18] *Ibid.*, 128.

liche (that which all thinking must presuppose). This *Un-vordenkliche* is not God, but it reveals itself as God to those who receive the revelation in some immediate crisis of experience. This revelation involves freedom on both sides; it is not a necessity of thought, like the idea of the "Absolute" taken as the highest concept of rational philosophy. In this fashion Schelling returns to Kant's critical position: God as God is an object of faith, and there is no rational realization of the idea of God. For pure thought God remains a mere possibility; on this Kant and Schelling agree. But then Schelling goes on to try to approach the God of revelation in terms of a third type of empiricism: "metaphysical empiricism"—a procedure that leads him to a speculative reinterpretation of the history of religion. The speculative urge in his mind conquered the Existential restriction and humility that he had himself postulated.

Although the philosophers of Existence denied Schelling's "metaphysical empiricism"—many of them were greatly disappointed by his Berlin lectures—they all demanded with him an "empirical" or experiential approach to Existence. And since they assumed that Existence is given immediately in the inner personal experience or concrete "Existence" of men, they all started with the immediate personal experience of the existing experiencer. They turned, not to the *thinking subject*, like Descartes, but to the *existing subject*—to the *"sum"* in *cogito ergo sum*, as Heidegger puts it. The description of this *sum*, of the character of immediate personal experience, is different for each representative of Existential philosophy. But on the basis of this personal experience each of them develops a theory in rational terms, a philosophy. They all try to "think Existence," to develop its implications, instead of simply living in "Existential" immediate experience.

Thus for Schelling the approach to Existence is through the

immediate personal experience of the Christian, the traditional faith—although rationally interpreted. For Kierkegaard it is the immediate personal experience of the individual in the face of eternity, his personal faith—although interpreted by a most refined dialectical reasoning. For Feuerbach it is the experience of man as man in his sense-existence—although developed into a doctrine of Man. For Marx it is the experience of the socially determined man, his Existence as a member of a social class—though interpreted in terms of a universal socio-economic theory. For Nietzsche it is the experience of a biologically determined being, his Existence as an embodiment of the Will to Power—although expressed in a metaphysics of Life. For Bergson it is the experience of dynamic vitality, man's Existence as duration and creativity—although expressed in words taken from the realm of non-existential space. For Dilthey it is the experience of the intellectual life, man's Existence in a special cultural situation—although explained in a universal *Geistesphilosophie*. For Jaspers it is the experience of the inner activity of the Self, man's Existence as "self-transcendence"—although described in terms of an immanent psychology. For Heidegger it is the experience of that kind of being who is "concerned" with Being, with his Existence as care, anxiety, and resoluteness—although Heidegger claims to describe the structure of Being itself. For the Religious Socialist it is the immediate personal experience of man's historical Existence, the pregnant historical moment—although expressed in a general interpretation of history.

6. The Existential thinker

The approach to Existence or Reality through immediate personal experience leads to the idea of the "Existential thinker," a term coined by Kierkegaard but applicable to all Existential philosophers. "The way of objective reflexion makes the subject accidental and thereby transforms his Existence into something impersonal—truth also becomes impersonal, and this impersonal character is precisely its objective validity; for all interest, like all decision, is rooted in personal experience."[19]

The Existential thinker is the interested or passionate thinker. Although Hegel applies the words "interest" and "passion" to those driving forces in history which the "cunning Idea" uses for its purposes, there is for him no problem of Existential thinking, because individuals are but the agents of the objective dialectical process. It is chiefly Marx who uses the term "interest" in this connection, though it is not lacking in Kierkegaard also. According to Marx, the Idea always fails when it is divorced from interest.[20] When united with interest, it can be either ideology or truth. It is "ideology" if, while claiming to represent society as a whole, it expresses merely the interest of a partial group. It is "true" if the partial group whose interest it expresses represents by its very nature the interest of the entire society. For Marx, in the period of capitalism this group is the proletariat. In this way he tries to unite universal validity with the concrete situation of the Existential thinker.

Feuerbach and Kierkegaard prefer the term "passion" for the attitude of the Existential thinker. In his beautifully written *Grundsätze der Philosophie der Zukunft*, Feuerbach says: "Do not wish to be a philosopher in contrast to being a man . . . do not think as a thinker . . . think as a living, real being . . . think in Existence."[21] "Love is passion, and only·

---

[19] Kierkegaard, *Concluding Unscientific Postscript*, 173.
[20] Marx, *Der Historische Materialismus*, I, 379.
[21] Feuerbach, *Grundsätze der Philosophie der Zukunft* (Zürich, 1843), 78.

passion is the mark of Existence."[22] In order to unite this attitude with the demand for objectivity, he says: "Only what is as an object of passion—really is."[23] The passionately living man knows the true nature of man and life.

Kierkegaard's famous definition of truth reads, "An objective uncertainty held fast in the most passionate personal experience is the truth, the highest truth attainable for an Existing individual."[24] This, he continues, is the definition of faith. Such a view seems to exclude any objective validity, and can hardly be considered the basis for an Existential philosophy. But Kierkegaard tries to show through the example of Socrates that the Existential thinker can be a philosopher. "The Socratic ignorance which Socrates held fast with the entire passion of his personal experience was thus an expression of the principle that the eternal truth is related to an existing individual."[25] The validity of the truth which appears in a passionate personal experience is based on the relation of the Eternal to the Existing individual.

The Existential thinker cannot have pupils in the ordinary sense. He cannot communicate any ideas, because *they* are *not* the truth he wants to teach. He can only create in his pupil by indirect communication that "Existential state" or personal experience out of which the pupil may think and act. Kierkegaard carries out this interpretation for Socrates. But all Existential philosophers have made similar statements—naturally, for if the approach to Existence is through personal experience, the only possibility of educating is to bring the pupil by indirect methods to a personal experience of his own Existence.

[22] *Ibid.*, 60.

[23] *Ibid.*, 60.

[24] Kierkegaard, *Postscript*, 182.

[25] *Ibid.*, 180.

Interest, passion, indirect communication—all these qualities of the Existential thinker are forcefully expressed in Nietzsche. In no respect is he more obviously a philosopher of experienced Existence than in his description of Existential thinking. None of the later Existential philosophers has approached him in this, though they all hold the same attitude. While in Marx objective validity is united with "Existential" personal experience because of the special situation of the proletariat, in Nietzsche it is the Master-man in general and his prophet in particular who stand in the favored place where validity and Existence coincide.

The Existential thinker needs special forms of expression, because personal Existence cannot be expressed in terms of objective experience. So Schelling uses the traditional religious symbols, Kierkegaard uses paradox, irony, and the pseudonym, Nietzsche the oracle, Bergson images and fluid concepts, Heidegger a mixture of psychological and ontological terms, Jaspers uses what he calls "ciphers," and the Religious Socialist uses concepts oscillating between immanence and transcendence. They all wrestle with the problem of personal or "non-objective" thinking and its expression—this is the calamity of the Existential thinker.

II. ONTOLOGICAL PROBLEMS OF THE EXISTENTIAL PHILOSOPHY

1. Existential immediacy and the subject-object distinction

The thinking of the Existential thinker is based on his immediate personal and inner experience. It is rooted in an interpretation of Being or Reality which does *not* identify Reality with "objective being." But it would be equally misleading to say that it identifies Reality with "Subjective being," with "consciousness" or feeling. Such a view would still leave the meaning of "subjective" determined by its contrast with "objective," and this is just the contrary of what the Existential philosophy is aiming at. Like many other appeals to immediate experience, it is trying to find a level on which the contrast between "subject" and "object" has not arisen. It aims to cut under the "subject-object distinction" and to reach that stratum of Being which Jaspers, for instance, calls the "*Ursprung*" or "Source." But in order to penetrate to this stratum we must leave the sphere of "objective" things and pass through the corresponding "subjective" inner experience, until we arrive at the immediate creative experience or "Source." " 'Existence' is something that can never become a mere object; it is the 'Source' whence springs my thinking and acting." [26] Schelling follows Hegel in emphasizing the "subject" and its freedom against Substance and its necessity. But while in Hegel the "subject" is immediately identified with the *thinking* subject, in Schelling it becomes rather the "*existing*" or immediately experiencing subject.

All the Existential philosophers reject any identification of Being or Reality with the objects of thought, which they feel is the great threat to personal human Existence in our period. Nietzsche writes in the third book of the *Will to Power*: "Knowledge and Becoming exclude each other. Consequently knowledge must signify something different. A 'will to make recognizable' must precede it; a special kind of

---

[26] Jaspers, *Philosophie*, I, 15.

becoming, man, must have created the deception of Being"[27]
—that is, of objective Being. All the categories establishing
the objective world are useful deceptions necessary for the
preservation of the human race. But the "Source," Life itself,
cannot be made into an object of thought by these categories.

For Bergson we lose our genuine Existence, our real nature,
if we think of ourselves in the "spatialized" terms appropriate
to objective things. "The moments in which we grasp ourselves
are rare, and consequently we are seldom free. Our existence is more in space than in time."[28] Real Existence, our
true nature, is the life in self-possession and duration.

According to Marx, "*Verdinglichung*," for men to become
"objects," things or commodities, is characteristic of the present world. But to be essentially human is just the opposite.
Natural forces and their transformation through technology
are really man's natural forces, they are man's objects, con-
firming *his* individuality. Industry is the secret revelation
of the powers of human nature.[29]

Jaspers declares that personal Existence ("Existential Subjectivity") is the center and aim of Reality. No being who
lacks such a personal experience can ever understand Existence. But those beings who do possess it can themselves
understand such defective and sub-human creatures to be the
result of a tragic loss of personal Existence. Heidegger denies
that it is possible to approach Being through objective reality,
and insists that "Existential Being," *Dasein*, self-relatedness,
is the only door to Being itself. The objective world ("*Das*

[27] Nietzsche, *Wille zur Macht* (1884–88); *Werke* (Taschenausgabe,
Leipzig, 1906), IX, 387.

[28] Bergson, *Essai sur les données immédiates de la conscience* (German tr., Jena, 1911), 182.

[29] Marx, *Der Historische Materialismus*, I, 301, 304.

Vorhandene") is a late product of immediate personal experience.

The meaning of this desperate refusal to identify Reality with the world of objects is clearly brought out by Nietzsche when he says: "When we have reached the inevitable universal economic administration of the earth, then mankind as a machine can find its meaning in the service of this monstrous mechanism of smaller and smaller cogs adapted to the whole." [30] No one any longer knows the significance of this huge process. Mankind demands a new aim, a new meaning for life. In these words anxiety about the social character of the "objective world" is clearly revealed as the motive for the fight of the philosophers of personal Existence against "objectivation," against the transformation of men into impersonal objects.

2. Psychological and ontological concepts

The principle of personal Existence or "Existential Subjectivity" demands a special type of concept in which to describe this immediate personal experience. These concepts must be "non-objectivating"; they must not transform men into things, but at the same time they must not be merely "subjective." In the light of this double demand we can understand the choice of psychological notions with a non-psychological connotation.

If the philosophy of personal Existence is right in maintaining that immediate experience is the door to the creative "Source" of Being, it is necessary for the concepts describing immediate experience to be at the same time descriptive of the structure of Being itself. The so-called "affects" are then not mere subjective emotions with no ontological significance;

[30] Nietzsche, *Wille zur Macht*, *Werke*, x, 114.

they are half-symbolic, half-realistic indications of the structure of Reality itself. It is in this way that Heidegger and many other philosophers of personal Existence are to be understood. Heidegger fills his book *Sein und Zeit* not with definitions of *Sein*-as-such or *Zeit*-as-such, but with descriptions of what he calls *Dasein* and *Zeitlichkeit*, temporal or finite Existence. In these descriptions he speaks of *Sorge* (care) as the general character of Existence, or of *Angst* (anxiety) as the relation of man to nothingness, or of fear of death, conscience, guilt, despair, daily life, loneliness, etc. But he insists again and again that these characterizations are not "ontic," describing merely a particular being, Man, but are rather "ontological," describing the very structure of Being itself. He denies that their negative character, their seemingly pessimistic connotations, have anything to do with actual pessimism. They all point to human finitude, the real theme of the philosophy of personal Existence. It remains, of course, an open question how the psychological meaning of these concepts can be distinguished from their ontological meaning. Most of the criticism directed against Heidegger deals with this problem; and it appears that Heidegger has implicitly admitted that he was unable to explain the difference clearly, and that he himself has increasingly emphasized human nature as the starting-point of the Existential ontology.

But this does not solve the problem. It is obvious that all the Existential philosophers and their predecessors have developed ontology in psychological terms. In Böhme, in Baader, in Schelling's *Human Freedom*, and in many other places, we find the belief in an essential relationship between human nature and Being, the belief that the innermost center of Nature lies in the heart of man. An especially important example of this ontological use of a psychological term is the conception of "Will" as the ultimate principle of Being. We find this in Böhme and in all those influenced by him, and before Böhme in Augustine, Duns Scotus, and Luther. Schelling's early view of the Will as *"Ur-Sein"* and his whole later voluntarism developed in his doctrine of Freedom, Nietzsche's symbol of the Will to Power, Bergson's *élan vital*, Schopenhauer's ontology of Will, the "Unconscious" of Hartmann and Freud—all these concepts of the non-rational are psychological notions with an ontological significance. The philosophers of Existence have used them, as well as other psychological concepts, to protect us from the annihilation of the "creative Source" by an "objective world" which was created out of that "Source" but which now is swallowing it like a monstrous mechanism.

3. The Principle of Finitude

In Hegel the whole world-process is explained in terms of the dialectical identity of the finite with the infinite. The Existential divorce of the finite from the infinite is entirely denied, not merely, as in mysticism, overcome in occasional ecstatic experiences. Kant's critical warning against such undue transgression of the limits of the finite mind is quite ignored.

The philosophy of experienced Existence re-establishes the consciousness of the divorce of the finite from the infinite. All the Existential philosophers strongly emphasize this point. Schelling, himself more responsible than anyone else for the victory of the Principle of Identity, and of intellectual intuition as the means of achieving it, later asserts that it is valid only in the realm of essence, not in that of existence. Kierkegaard follows Schelling: "The rationalistic Idea is the Identity of subject and object, the unity of thought and Being. Exis-

tence, on the other hand, is their separation."[31] With respect
to finitude he says: "Existence is a synthesis of the infinite and
the finite."[32] But this synthesis is just the opposite of Identity.
It is the basis of Existential despair, of the will to get rid of
oneself. Despair is the expression of the relation of separation
in this synthesis; it reveals the dynamic insecurity of the spirit.
Jaspers' description of the "boundary-situations," our historical relativity, death, suffering, struggle, guilt, points in the
same direction. Especially strong is the idea of finitude expressed in his doctrine of the necessary *Scheitern* (shipwreck)
of the finite in its relation to the infinite. "Since Personal Existence tries in the process of becoming to transcend the
measure of its finitude, the finite being ... is finally ruined."[33]

Feuerbach says: "The subject which has nothing outside
itself, and therefore no limits within itself, has ceased to be a
finite subject."[34] Marx describes man as a being related to
objects through want, sensuality, activity, suffering, and passion. Nietzsche's pragmatic view of knowledge as well as
his longing for eternity shows his consciousness of our finitude
in thinking and being.

But most important in this connection is Heidegger's attempt to interpret Kant's critical philosophy in terms of
Existential philosophy, primarily in terms of human finitude.
In his *Kant and the Problem of Metaphysics* (1929) he intro-
duces the subject of his inquiry as Kant's attempt to found
metaphysics on the human, that is, the finite, character of
reason.[35]

Finitude is the very structure of the human mind, to be
distinguished from mere shortcomings, error, or accidental

[31] Kierkegaard, *Concluding Unscientific Postscript*, 112.
[32] *Ibid.*, 350.
[33] Jaspers, *Philosophie*, III, 229.
[34] Feuerbach, *Grundsätze*, 39.
[35] p. 19.

limitations. While for Kant God—as a mere ideal—has an infinite "intuition," man has a finite intuition, and therefore needs to employ discursive thinking. "The character of the finitude of intuition is its receptivity."[36] Therefore, finite knowledge has "objects"—the definition of finitude in Feuerbach and Marx, with which Dilthey's interpretation of reality as resistance may be compared. For Heidegger, Kant's epistemological problem is: "How must that finite being we call man be equipped in order to be aware of a kind of Being which is not the same as he himself?"[37] The several chapters of the *Kritik* answer this question step by step. "The revelation of the structure of the 'pure synthesis' reveals the very nature of the finitude of reason."[38]

While an ontology which claims to have knowledge of Being *a priori* is arrogant, an ontology which restricts itself to the structure of finitude is possible.[39] Such an ontology can be called a doctrine of human nature, but not in the sense of giving any special knowledge of the human race. An ontological doctrine of man develops the structure of finitude as man finds it in himself as the center of his own personal Existence. He alone of all finite beings is aware of his own finitude; therefore the way to ontology passes through the doctrine of man. But of course, in traveling this way he cannot escape his finitude. The way to finitude is itself finite and cannot claim finality: such is the limit set upon the Existential thinker. Heidegger concludes his analysis with the statement that the fight against Kant's doctrine of the *Ding-an-sich* was a fight against the acknowledgment of the finitude of our human experience in knowing.

[36] *Ibid.*, 23.
[37] *Ibid.*, 39.
[38] *Ibid.*, 66.
[39] *Ibid.*, 118.

4. Time as "Existential" or immediately experienced, and Time as measured

For the whole of Existential philosophy the analysis of finitude culminates in the analysis of Time. The insight that existence is distinguished from essence by its temporal character is as old as the philosophy of Existence. An essay on the doctrine of Time in the different philosophers of Existence, their agreements and their differences, would be a worthwhile task. But we must confine ourselves to a few suggestions.

The general tendency is to distinguish "Existential" or immediately experienced Time from dialectical timelessness on the one hand, and from the infinite, quantitative, measured Time of the objective world, on the other. That qualitative Time is characteristic of Personal Experience is the general theme of the Existential philosophy. In his *Weltalter* Schelling distinguishes three qualitatively different kinds of Time: the pre-temporal, the temporal, and the post-temporal; he tries to escape from infinite progress and regress by assuming a beginning and an end. Kierkegaard seeks to escape from measured and objective Time through his doctrine of the *Augenblick*, the pregnant moment in which Eternity touches Time and demands a personal decision. Secondly, he tries to avoid the objectivity of the Past through his idea of "*Gleichzeitigkeit*," which takes all history to be contemporaneous with the pregnant moment, and claims that a repetition of the Past is a present possibility. Nietzsche escapes from infinite, quantitative Time through his doctrine of "eternal recurrence" which gives to every moment the weight of eternity, and through his eschatological division of Time in the symbol of the "Great Noon."

Marx's distinction between pre-history and history tries to introduce a definite qualitative element into the course of quantitative Time. Religious Socialism, through its doctrine of the "center of history" which determines the beginning and the end of "historical Time," and through its idea of "time fulfilled" or the *Kairos*, has tried to go in the same direction of transcending quantitative through qualitative Time. Bergson's fight against quantitative and objective Time, in which Time is subjected to Space, belongs to the same line of development.

The most radical of these efforts is Heidegger's distinction between "Existential" and objective Time. No one has emphasized so strongly as he the identity between experienced Existence and temporality: "Temporality is the genuine meaning of Care,"[40] and Care is finite Existence. Heidegger carries through this idea with respect to the whole structure of experienced Existence, especially in connection with the anticipation of our own death, which generates the way in which we can grasp ourselves as a whole. In his analysis of Kant he indicates that for himself Time is defined by "self-affection," grasping oneself or one's Personal Existence. Temporality is Existentiality. In distinction from this qualitative Time, objective Time is the Time of the flight from our own Personal Existence into the universal "one," the "everyone," the average human Existence, in which quantitative measurement is necessary and justified. But this universal Time is not *eigentlich* or proper; it is Time objectified, and it must be interpreted in the light of Existential Time, Time as immediately experienced, and not vice versa.

[40] Heidegger, *Sein und Zeit* (Halle, 1927), 326.

III. THE ETHICAL ATTITUDE OF THE
EXISTENTIAL PHILOSOPHY

1. History viewed in the light of the future

All the Existential philosophers agree on the historical character of immediate personal experience. But the fact that man has a fundamentally "historical Existence" does not mean merely that he has a theoretical interest in the past; his Existence is not directed toward the past at all. It is the attitude not of the detached spectator, but of the actor who must face the future and make personal decisions.

Schelling calls his positive philosophy "historical philosophy," because being "historical" means for him being open for the future. Since the revelation of *das Unvordenkliche* is never completed, the positive philosophy is never finished. We have already touched on Kierkegaard's doctrines of the "pregnant moment," of contemporaneity and repetition, as well as on the use made of these ideas by German Religious Socialism to interpret history. For Marx man's experience is fundamentally conditioned by the historical and cultural setting of his life. Human nature is itself historical, and cannot be understood without an understanding of its present stage of dehumanization, and of the demand for a "real humanism" in the future. Philosophical doctrines of human nature and of ontology are dependent on the revolutionary achievement in the future of what man has the power to make of himself.

In his second *Unzeitgemässe Betrachtungen* Nietzsche states emphatically the historical character of human experience. "The word of the past is always an oracle uttered. Only as builders of the future, as knowing the present, will you understand it."[41] In this Heidegger follows Nietzsche: The his-

[41] Nietzsche, *Unzeitgemässe Betrachtungen*, *Werke*, II, 161.

torical character of human experience lies in its orientation toward the future. Mere historical knowledge is not man's real role as an historical being. Absorption in the past is an estrangement from our task as the makers of history.[42]

2. Finitude and estrangement

The description of man's "Existential situation" or present estate as finitude is usually connected with the contrast between man's present estate and what he is "essentially," and therefore ought to be. Ever since Schelling's *On Human Freedom*, the world we are living in, including Nature, has been described as a disrupted unity, as fragments and ruins. In accord with Kant's half-mythological and genuinely "Existential" doctrine of radical evil, Schelling speaks of the transcendent Fall of Man as the "presupposition of the tragic nature of Existence." Kierkegaard's famous work on *Angst*, in which he interprets the transition from essence to existence, is his psychological masterpiece: the *Angst* of finitude drives man to action and at the same time to an alienation from his essential being and to the profounder *Angst* of guilt and despair.

Both Schelling and Kierkegaard aim to distinguish "finitude" from "alienation" or "estrangement." But neither really succeeds; the finite character of immediate personal experience makes the "Fall" practically inescapable. Nietzsche, Heidegger, Jaspers, and Bergson do not even try to make a distinction. They describe immediate experience in terms of both finitude *and* guilt—that is, in tragic terms. *Verfallenheit*, being lost and a prey to the necessity of existing, constitutes guilt. As Heidegger says, "Being guilty is not the result of a

42 Heidegger, *Sein und Zeit*, 396.

guilty act, but conversely, the act is possible only because of an original 'being guilty.' "[43] The tragic interpretation of life which has prevailed among the European intelligentsia during the last decades is not unrelated to the Existential philosophy.

Marx described the situation of dehumanization and self-estrangement in innumerable fragments. One of the most precious pieces is his description of the function of money as the main symbol of self-estrangement or alienation in present society. But estrangement is not for him an inevitable tragic necessity. It is the product of a special historical situation, and can be overcome through human action. It is in this attitude that the Utopian elements of the later Marxist movements are rooted. But the subsequent history of these movements has shown that Marx's description of man as a passionate and suffering being holds true even after a victorious revolution. The relation between finitude and estrangement is fundamental for Existential philosophy.

3. Finitude and loneliness

Every personal Existence is unique, says Jaspers: "We are completely irreplaceable. We are not merely cases of universal Being."[44] Heidegger speaks of the *Jemeinigkeit* of personal Existence, its belonging to me and nobody else.[45] Men usually live in the common experiences of daily life, covering over with talk and action their real inner personal experience. But conscience, guilt, having to die, come home to the individual only in his inner loneliness. The death of another as an ob-

---

[43] Heidegger, *Sein und Zeit*, 284.

[44] Jaspers, *Vernunft und Existenz* (Groningen, 1935), 19.

[45] Heidegger, *Sein und Zeit*, 42.

jective event has nothing to do with our personal attitude toward our own death. Nietzsche praises the higher type of man who is lonely and cut off not only from the masses but also from others like himself. Nietzsche's estimate of the average man is exactly that of Heidegger and Jaspers. Kierkegaard goes even beyond them in emphasizing man's inner experience of loneliness before God. Anything objective and universal has no other meaning for him than an escape from the ethical decision each individual has to make.

Feuerbach and Marx seem to diverge on this point from the other philosophers of Human Existence. Feuerbach makes a very profound comment on the problem of loneliness: "True dialectic is not a monologue of the lonely thinker with himself. It is a dialogue between the Ego and the Thou."[46] This Ego-Thou philosophy has had great influence on present-day German theology since Buber and Griesebach. But the question is, what can we substitute for this inner loneliness? Without such an alternative the Ego-Thou relation remains a mere form. This is implied in Marx's criticism of Feuerbach, that he knows man in the abstract, and man the individual, but not man the social being. Marx himself sees only this social man. But he there discovers man's estrangement, which is not only man's estrangement from himself but also from every other man. For him, this loneliness arises from present historical conditions which must be transformed. But the struggle to create true humanity in the proletariat has led in actual fact not to "community," but only to "solidarity," a relation which is still external and remains a symbol of man's estrangement.

In all the Existential philosophers it is this loss of community that has provoked the flight from the objective world. Only in that world—in what Heraclitus called "the common world

[46] Feuerbach, *Grundsätze*, 83.

in which we live our waking lives"—is genuine community between man and man possible. If this common world has disappeared or grown intolerable, the individual turns to his lonely inner experience, where he is forced to spin out dreams which isolate him still further from this world, even though his objective knowledge of it may be very extensive. Here is suggested much of the social background of the philosophy of Human Existence.

CONCLUSION—THE SIGNIFICANCE OF THE EXISTENTIAL PHILOSOPHY

We have considered a large group of Existential philosophers, covering a period of about a hundred years. They represent many different and even contradictory tendencies in philosophic thought, and they had many different and even contradictory effects on religion and politics. Do they all exhibit some common trait which justifies calling them all "Existential philosophers"? If the above analysis is correct, there can be no doubt that they display a very fundamental unity. This unity can be described in both negative and positive terms: all the philosophers of Existence share a common opposition to a common foe, and all have a common aim, though they try to attain it in very different ways.

What all philosophers of Existence oppose is the "rational" system of thought and life developed by Western industrial society and its philosophic representatives. During the last hundred years the implications of this system have become increasingly clear: a logical or naturalistic mechanism which seemed to destroy individual freedom, personal decision, and organic community; an analytic rationalism which saps the vital forces of life and transforms everything, including man himself, into an object of calculation and control; a secularized humanism which cuts man and the world off from the creative Source and the ultimate mystery of existence. The Existential philosophers, supported by poets and artists in every European country, were consciously or subconsciously aware of the approach of this self-estranged form of life. They tried to resist it in a desperate struggle which drove them often to mental self-destruction and made their utterances extremely aggressive, passionate, paradoxical, fragmentary, revolutionary, prophetic, and ecstatic. But this did not prevent them from achieving fundamental insights into the sociological structure of modern society and the psychological dynamics of modern man, into the originality and spontaneity of life, into the paradoxical character of religion and the Existential roots of knowledge. They immensely enriched philosophy, if it be taken as man's interpretation of his own existence, and they worked out intellectual tools and spiritual symbols for the European revolution of the twentieth century.

To understand the fundamental drive and function of Existential philosophy, it is necessary to view it against the background of what was happening in the nineteenth-century religious situation, especially in Germany, for all the groups that appeared after 1830 had to face a common problem, the problem created by the breakdown of the religious tradition under the impact of enlightenment, social revolution, and bourgeois liberalism. First among the educated classes, then increasingly in the mass of industrial workers, religion lost its "immediacy," it ceased to offer an unquestioned sense of direction and relevance to human living. What was lost in immediacy Hegel tried to restore by conscious reinterpretation. But this mediating reinterpretation was attacked and dissolved from both sides by a revived theology on the one hand and by philosophical positivism on the other. The Existential philosophers were trying to discover an ultimate meaning of life beyond the reach of reinterpretation, revived theologies, or positivism. In their search they passionately rejected the "estranged" objective world with its religious radicals, reactionaries, and mediators. They turned toward man's immediate experience, toward "subjectivity," not as something opposed to "objectivity," but as that living experience in which both objectivity and subjectivity are rooted. They turned toward Reality as men experience it immediately in their actual living, to *Innerlichkeit* or inward experience. They tried to discover the creative realm of being which is prior to and beyond the distinction between objectivity and subjectivity.

If the experience of this level of living is "mystical," Existential philosophy can be called the attempt to reconquer the meaning of life in "mystical" terms after it had been lost in ecclesiastical as well as in positivistic terms. It is however necessary to redefine "mystical" if we are to apply it to Existential philosophy. In this context the term does not indicate a mystical union with the transcendent Absolute; it signifies rather a venture of faith toward union with the depths of life, whether made by an individual or a group. There is more of the Protestant than the Catholic heritage in this kind of "mysticism"; but it *is* mysticism in trying to transcend the estranged "objectivity" as well as the empty "subjectivity" of the present epoch. Historically speaking, Existential philosophy attempts to return to a pre-Cartesian attitude, to an attitude in which the sharp gulf between the subjective and the objective "realms" had not yet been created, and the essence of objectivity could be found in the depth of subjectivity—in which God could be best approached through the soul.

This problem and this solution are in some respects peculiar to the German situation, in others common to all European culture. It is the desperate struggle to find a new meaning of life in a reality from which men have been estranged, in a cultural situation in which two great traditions, the Christian and the humanistic, have lost their comprehensive character and their convincing power. The turning towards *Inner-lichkeit*, or more precisely, toward the creative sources of life in the depth of man's experience, occurred throughout Europe. For sociological reasons it was in Germany more philosophical and more radical than in other lands. There it became that quasi-religious power which had transformed society, first in Russia and then in other parts of Europe, during the first half of the twentieth century.

In understanding Existential philosophy a comparison with the situation in England may be helpful. England is the only European country in which the Existential problem of finding a new meaning for life had no significance, because there positivism and the religious tradition lived on side by side, united by a social conformism which prevented radical questions about the meaning of human "Existence." It is important to note that the one country without an Existential philosophy is that in which during the period from 1830 to 1930 the religious tradition remained strongest. This illustrates once more the dependence of the Existential philosophy on the problems created by the breakdown of the religious tradition on the European continent.

In their struggle against the meaninglessness of modern technological civilization, the several philosophers of Existence used very different methods and had very different aims. In all of them the Existential emphasis was only one factor among others, more or less controlling. Schelling shared the belief of German Romanticism that a new philosophy, and in particular a new interpretation of religion, could produce a new reality.

But this assumption was wrong; and his immediate influence remained very limited, restricted to the theology of the restoration period. Feuerbach's significance for Existential thinking lies more in his destruction of Hegel's reconciliation of Christianity with modern philosophy than in his metaphysical materialism, which indeed considerably strengthened the bourgeois-mechanistic interpretation of nature and man.

Kierkegaard represents the religious wing of Existential philosophy. He himself did not claim to be a philosopher, and those who find in him the classic type of Existential thinking often assert that a genuinely Existential thinker cannot be one. But Kierkegaard's actual work reveals a much more intimate connection. As a religious thinker he encountered the obstacle of a church which had become "bourgeois" in both theory and practice, and he was able to maintain his own radical Christianity only in terms of an absolute paradox and of a passionately personal devotion. As a philosophical thinker, however, he produced a "dialectical" psychology which has contributed greatly to an anti-rationalistic and anti-mechanistic interpretation of human nature.

If we call Marx an Existential thinker, this can obviously apply only to certain particular strains of his thought: to his struggle against the self-estrangement of man under capitalism, against any theory that merely interprets the world without changing it, against the assumption that knowledge is quite independent of the social situation in which it is sought. Like Kierkegaard, Marx did not want to be a philosopher: he pronounced the end of all philosophy and its transformation into a revolutionary sociology. But the impulse he gave to the interpretation of history, his doctrine of "ideology," his introduction of sociological analysis into economics, made him a powerful force in the philosophic discussion of the end of the nineteenth and the beginning of the twentieth centuries, long before he became the greatest political force in the fight of the twentieth century against the traditions of the nineteenth.

Like Marx, Nietzsche and the *"Lebensphilosophen"* are Existential philosophers only in certain of their views. Nietzsche's attack on "European nihilism," his biological interpretation of the categories of knowledge, his fragmentary and prophetic style, his eschatological passion; Dilthey's problem of the Existential roots of the different interpretations of life; Bergson's attack on spatial rationality in the name of creative vitality; the primacy of life as over against its products in Simmel and Scheler—all these ideas reveal their Existential character. But just as Marx never called into question natural science, economic theory, and dialectical reason, so Nietzsche and the *"Lebensphilosophen"* always presupposed the scientific method and an ontology of life. Heidegger, and less emphatically Jaspers, returned to the Kierkegaardian type of Existential philosophy, and in particular to the dialectical psychology of Kierkegaard. They reintroduced the term "Existential" to designate a philosophy that appealed to immediate personal experience, and they cooperated with a theology that was profoundly influenced by Kierkegaard, especially by his attack on the secularized bourgeois churches. But with the help of Aristotle and the *"Lebensphilosophie,"* Heidegger transformed the dialectical psychology into a new ontology, radically rejecting the religious implications of the Existential attitude, and replacing it with the unchecked resoluteness of the tragic and heroic individual.

It is a dramatic picture that Existential philosophy presents: the polarity between the Existential attitude and its philosophic expression dominates the whole movement. At times the Existential element prevails, at times the philosophical—even in the same thinker. In all of them the critical interest is predominant. All of them are reacting—in theory and practice—against an historical destiny the fulfilment of which they are furthering by their very reaction against it. They are the expression of the great revolution within and against Western industrial society which was prepared in the nineteenth century and is being carried out in the twentieth.

VIII

The Theological Significance of
Existentialism and Psychoanalysis

WE SHALL be using the two words psychoanalysis and theology. By their very nature they pose semantic problems for us. Psychoanalysis can be a special term, and it is often usurped by the Freudian school, which declares that no other school has a right to use the term. A recent conversation with a representative of this school moved cordially up to the moment when people like Horney, Fromm, Jung, and Rank were called psychoanalysts. At this moment the Freudian broke in and said, "They are dishonest in calling themselves psychoanalysts. They shouldn't do it. They do it only for purposes of profit."

This situation shows that we have to do something about this term. It is not used here as this psychoanalyst used it, but rather in the meaning into which this term has been transformed and enlarged during the last half-century. These developments surely are dependent on the basic Freudian discovery, namely, the role of the unconscious. However, there are two other words which indicate something about the matter itself and could be used here: "therapeutic psychology" is one term often used, and another is "depth psychology."

About the term theology, perhaps many of you know that in our theological seminaries and divinity schools, the word theology often is used exclusively for systematic theology, and that historical and practical theology are not considered theology at all. We will enlarge the concept of theology for our discussion of its relationship to depth psychology and include in it past religious movements and great religious figures, and also the New Testament writings. Also, we want to include practical theology, where the relationship to psychoanalysis has become most conspicuous, namely, in the function of the counsellor who gives counsel in religious and in psychoanalytic terms at the same time.

Then we must also discuss the gap that has developed in the relation of existentialism to psychoanalysis. This is a real gap, because existentialism is now taken in a much broader sense than it was a few years after the Second World War. At that time existentialism was identified with the philosophy of Sartre. But existentialism appears in decisive forms early in the 17th and in the 19th centuries, and it is incorporated in almost all great creations in all areas of life in the 20th century. If you understand existentialism in this broader sense, it suggests very definitely a relationship between existentialism and psychoanalysis. A basic assertion to be made about the relationship of theology and psychoanalysis is that pychoanalysis belongs fundamentally to the whole existentialist movement of the 20th century, and that as a part of this movement it must be understood in its relationship to theology in the same way in which the relationship of existentialism generally must be understood.

This factor reveals something about the philosophical implications of depth psychology, and also about the interdependence between this movement and the existentialist movement of the 19th and 20th centuries. It is a fact that psychoanalysis and existentialism have been connected with each other from the very beginning; they have mutually influenced each other in the most radical and profound ways.

Everybody who has looked into the works of existentialist writers from Dostoyevsky on to the present will immediately agree that there is much depth-psychological material in the novels, the dramas, and the poems, as well as in the visual arts— modern art being the existentialist form of visual art. All this is understandable only if we see that there is a common root and intention in existentialism and psychoanalysis.

If these common roots are found, the question of the relationship of psychoanalysis and theology is brought into a larger and more fundamental framework. Then it is possible to reject the attempts of some theologians and some psychologists to divide these two realms carefully and give to each of them a special sphere. It is then possible to disregard those people who tell us to stay in this or that field: here a system of theological doctrines and there congeries of psychological insights. This is not so. The relationship is not one of existing alongside each other; it is a relationship of mutual inter-penetration.

The common root of existentialism and psychoanalysis is the protest against the increasing power of the philosophy of consciousness in modern industrial society. This conflict between the philosophy of consciousness and the protest against it is of course much older than modern industrial society. It appeared in the 13th century in the famous conflict between the primacy of the intellect in Thomas Aquinas and the primacy of the irrational will in Duns Scotus. Both of these men were theologians, and I mention them mainly in order to show how untenable theological positions are which want to exclude philosophical and psychological problems from theology. The struggle between these two basic attitudes towards not only the nature of man but also the nature of God and the world has continued ever since.

In the Renaissance, we have philosophers of consciousness,

for instance, humanists of the type of Erasmus of Rotterdam or scientists of the type of Galileo. But against them stood others, as for instance, Paracelsus in the realm of medical philosophy who fought against the anatomical mechanization of medicine and against the separation of body and mind, or Jacob Boehme, who influenced the subsequent period very much, particularly by his description in mythological terms of the unconscious elements in the ground of the divine life itself and therefore of all life. We find the same conflict in the Reformation: on the one hand the victory of consciousness in reformers like Melanchthon, Zwingli, and Calvin, all of them dependent on humanists of the Erasmus type, while the irrational will was emphasized by Luther, on whom Jacob Boehme was largely dependent.

The history of industrial society, the end of which we are experiencing, represents the history of the victory of the philosophy of consciousness over the philosophy of the unconscious, irrational will. The symbolic name for the complete victory of the philosophy of consciousness is René Descartes; and the victory became complete, even in religion, at the moment when Protestant theology became the ally of the Cartesian emphasis on man as pure consciousness on the one hand, and a mechanical process called body on the other hand. In Lutheranism it was especially the cognitive side of man's consciousness which overwhelmed the early Luther's understanding of the irrational will. In Calvin it was the moral consciousness, the moral self-controlling center of consciousness that predominated. We have in America, which is mostly dependent on Calvinism and related outlooks, the moralistic and oppressive types of Protestantism which are the result of the complete victory of the philosophy of consciousness in modern Protestantism. But in spite of this victory, the protest was not silenced.

Pascal in the 17th century stood in conscious opposition to Descartes. His was the first existentialist analysis of the human situation, and he described it in ways very similar to those of later existentialist and non-existentialist philosophers, that is, in terms of anxiety, of finitude, of doubt, of guilt, of meaninglessness, of a world in which Newtonian atoms and cosmic bodies move according to mechanical laws; and as we know from many utterances, man decentralized, deprived of the earth as center, felt completely lost in this mechanized universe, in anxiety and meaninglessness. There were others in the 18th century; for example, Hamann, who is very little known outside of Germany, a kind of prophetic spirit anticipating many of the existentialist ideas. But the most radical protest came at the moment when the philosophy of consciousness reached its peak in the philosophy of Hegel. Against this victorious philosophy of consciousness Schelling arose, giving to Kierkegaard and many others the basic concepts of existentialism; then Schopenhauer's irrational will, Hartmann's philosophy of the unconscious, Nietzsche's analysis which anticipated most of the results of later depth-psychological inquiries. The protest appeared also in Kierkegaard's and Marx's description of the human predicament, in finitude, estrangement, and loss of subjectivity. And in Dostoyevsky we find the description of the demonic subconscious in man; we find it also in French poetry of the type of Rimbaud and Baudelaire. This was the preparation of the ground for what was to follow in the 20th century.

All the things which in these men were ontological intuition or theological analysis now through Freud became methodological scientific words. Freud, in his discovery of the unconscious, rediscovered something that was known long before, and had been used for many decades and even centuries to fight the victorious philosophy of consciousness. What

Freud did was to give to this protest a scientific methodological foundation. In him we must see the old protest against the philosophy of consciousness. Especially in men like Heidegger and Sartre, and in the whole literature and art of the 20th century, the existentialist point of view became aware of itself. It now was expressed intentionally and directly, and not only as a suppressed element of protest.

This short survey shows the inseparability of depth psychology from philosophy, and of both of them from theology. It is also clear that they cannot be separated if we now compare depth psychology and existentialist philosophy in their differences and in their similarities. The basic point is that both existentialism and depth psychology are interested in the description of man's existential predicament—in time and space, in finitude and estrangement—in contrast to man's essential nature, for if you speak of man's existential predicament as opposite to his essential nature, you must in some way presuppose an idea of his essential nature. But this is not the purpose to which all existentialist literature is directed. Instead, the focus in both existentialism and depth psychology is man's estranged existence, the characteristics and symptoms of this estrangement, and the conditions of existence in time and space. The term "therapeutic psychology" shows clearly that here something that contradicts the norm, that must be healed, is expressed. It shows the relation between disease—mental, bodily, or psychosomatic—and man's existential predicament.

It is also clear that all existential utterances deal with the boundary line between healthy and sick and ask one question —you can reduce it to this—how is it possible that a being has a structure that produces psychosomatic diseases? Existentialism in order to answer these questions points to the possible experience of meaninglessness, to the continuous experience of loneliness, to the widespread feeling of emptiness. It derives them from finitude, from the awareness of finitude which is anxiety; it derives them from estrangement from oneself and one's world. It points to the possibility and the danger of freedom, and to the threat of non-being in all respects—from death to guilt. All these are characteristic of man's existential predicament, and in this, depth psychology and existentialism agree.

However, there is a basic difference between them. Existentialism as philosophy speaks of the universal human situation, which refers to everybody, healthy or sick. Depth psychology points to the ways in which people try to escape the situation by fleeing into neurosis and falling into psychosis. In existentialist literature, not only in novels and poems and dramas but even in philosophy, it is difficult to distinguish clearly the boundary line between man's universal existential situation based on finitude and estrangement on the one hand, and man's psychosomatic disease which is considered an attempt to escape from this situation and its anxieties by fleeing into a mental fortress.

Now how are theological judgments applied to depth psychology and existentialism (which are in reality one thing). The relation between man's essential nature and his existential predicament is the first and basic question that theology has asked whenever it encounters existentialist analyses and psychoanalytic material. In the Christian tradition, there are three fundamental concepts. First: *Esse qua esse bonum est.* This Latin phrase is a basic dogma of Christianity. It means "Being as being is good," or in the biblical mythological form: God saw everything that he had created, and behold, it was good. The second statement is the universal fall—fall meaning the transition from this essential goodness into existential estrangement from oneself, which happens in every living being and in every time. The third statement refers to the possibility of salvation. We should remember that salvation is derived from *salvus* or *salus* in Latin, which means "healed" or "whole," as opposed to disruptiveness.

These three considerations of human nature are present in all genuine theological thinking: essential goodness, existential estrangement, and the possibility of something, a "third," beyond essence and existence, through which the cleavage is overcome and healed. Now, in philosophical terms, this means that man's essential and existential nature points to his teleological nature (derived from *telos*, aim, that for which and towards which his life drives).

If you do not distinguish these three elements, which are always present in man, you will fall into innumerable confusions. Every criticism of existentialism and psychoanalysis on the basis of this tripartite view of human nature is directed against the confusion of these three fundamental elements, which always must be distinguished although they always are together in all of us. Freud, in this respect, was unclear, namely, he was not able to distinguish man's essential and existential nature. This is a basic theological criticism, not of any special result of his thinking, but of his doctrine of man and the central intuition he has of man. His thought about libido makes this deficiency very obvious.

Man, according to him, as infinite libido which never can be satisfied and which therefore produces the desire to get rid of oneself, the desire he has called the death instinct. And this is not only true of the individual, it is also true of man's relation to culture as a whole. His dismay about culture shows that he is very consistent in his negative judgments about man as existentially distorted. Now if you see man only from the point of view of existence and not from the point of view of essence, only from the point of view of estrangement and not from the point of view of essential goodness, then this consequence is unavoidable. And it is true for Freud in this respect.

Let us make this clear by means of a theological concept which is very old, the classical concept of concupiscence. This concept is used in Christian theology exactly as libido is used by Freud, but it is used for man under the conditions of existence; it is the indefinite striving beyond any given satisfaction, to induce satisfaction beyond the given one. But according to theological doctrine, man in his essential goodness is not in the state of concupiscence or indefinite libido. Rather he is directed to a definite special subject, to content, to somebody, to something with which he is connected in love, or *eros*, or *agape*, whatever it may be. If this is the case, then the situation is quite different. Then you can have libido, but the fulfilled libido is real fulfillment, and you are not driven beyond this indefinitely. This means that Freud's description of libido is to be viewed theologically as the description of man in his existential self-estrangement. But Freud does not know any other man, and this is the basic criticism that theology would weigh against him on this point.

Now, fortunately, Freud, like most great men, was not consistent. With respect to the healing process, he knew something about the healed man, man in the third form, teleological man. And in so far as he was thus convinced of the possibility of healing, this contradicted profoundly his fundamental restriction to existential man. In popular terms, his pessimism about the nature of man and his optimism about the possibilities of healing were never reconciled in him or in his followers.

But some of his followers have done something else. They have rejected the profound insight of Freud about existential libido and the death instinct, and in so doing they have reduced and cut off from Freud what made him and still makes him the most profound of all the depth psychologists. This can be said even in relation to Jung, who is much more religiously interested than was Freud. But Freud, theologically speaking, saw more about human nature than all his followers who, when they lost the existentialist element in Freud, went more to an essentialist and optimistic view of man.

We can make the same criticism of Sartre's pure existentialism and his sensitive psychological analysis. The greatness of this man is that he is the psychological interpreter of Heidegger. He is perhaps misinterpreted on many points, but nevertheless his psychological insights are profound. But here we have the same thing that we have found before: Sartre says man's essence is his existence. In saying this he makes it impossible for man to be saved or to be healed. Sartre knows this, and every one of his plays shows this too. But here also we have a happy inconsistency. He calls his existentialism humanism. But if he calls it humanism, that means he has an idea of what man essentially is, and he must consider the possibility that the essential being of man, his freedom, might be lost. And if this is a possibility, then he makes, against his own will, a distinction between man as he essentially is and man as he can be lost: man is to be free and to create himself.

We have the same problem in Heidegger. Heidegger talks also as if there were no norms whatsoever, no essential man, as if man makes himself. On the other hand, he speaks of the difference between authentic existence and unauthentic existence, falling into the average existence of conventional thought and nonsense—into an existence where he has lost himself. This is very interesting, because it shows that even the most radical existentialist, if he wants to say something, necessarily falls back to some essentialist statements because without them he cannot even speak.

Other psychoanalysts have described the human situation

as correctible and amendable, as a weakness only. But we can ask: is man essentially healthy? If he is, only his basic anxiety has to be taken away; for example, if you save him from the evil influences of society, of competition and things like that, everything will be all right. Men like Fromm speak of the possibility of becoming an autonomous non-authoritarian personality who develops himself according to reason. And even Jung, who knows so much about the depths of the human soul and about the religious symbols, thinks that there are essential structures in the human soul and that it is possible (and one may be successful) to search for personality.

In all these representatives of contemporary depth psychology we miss the depths of Freud. We miss the feeling for the irrational element that we have in Freud and in much of the existentialist literature. Dostoyevsky has already been mentioned. We could also mention Kafka and many others.

Now we come to the third element, namely, the teleological, the element of fufillment, the question of healing. Here we have the difference between the healing of an acute illness and the healing of the existential presuppositions of every disease and of every healthy existence. This is the basis for the healing of special acute illnesses; on this all groups agree. There are acute illnesses that produce psychosomatic irregularities and destruction. There are compulsive restrictions of man's potentialities which lead to neurosis and eventually to psychosis. But beyond this there are the existential presuppositions. Neither Freudianism nor any purely existentialist consideration can heal these fundamental presuppositions. Many psychoanalysts try to do it. They try with their methods to overcome existential negativity, anxiety, estrangement, meaninglessness, or guilt. They deny that they are universal, that they are existential in this sense. They call all anxiety, all guilt, all emptiness, illnesses which can be overcome as any illness can be, and they try to remove them. But this is impossible. The existential structures cannot be healed by the most refined techniques. They are objects of salvation. The analyst can be an instrument of salvation as every friend, every parent, every child can be an instrument of salvation. But as analyst he cannot bring salvation by means of his medical methods, for this requires the healing of the center of the personality. So much for the criticism.

Now how can theology deal with depth psychology? Certainly the growth of the two movements, existentialism and depth psychology, is of infinite value for theology. Both of them brought to theology something which it always should have known but which it had forgotten and covered up. They helped to rediscover the immense depth psychological material which we find in the religious literature of the last two thousand years and even beyond that. Almost every insight concerning the movement of the soul can be found in this literature, and the most classical example of all is perhaps Dante's *Divine Comedy*, especially in the description of hell and purgatory, and of the inner self-destructiveness of man in his estrangement from his essential being.

Second, it was a rediscovery of the meaning of the word "sin" which had become entirely unintelligible by the identification of sin with sins, and by the identification of sins with certain acts that are not conventional or not approvable. Sin is something quite different. It is universal, tragic estrangement, based on freedom and destiny in all human beings, and should never be used in the plural. Sin is separation, estrangement from one's essential being. That is what it means; and if this is the result of depth psychological work, then this of course is a great gift that depth psychology and existentialism have offered to theology.

Thirdly, depth psychology has helped theology to rediscover the demonic structures that determine our consciousness and our decisions. Again, this is very important. It means that if we believe we are free in terms of conscious decision, we can find that something has happened to us which directed these decisions before we made them. The illusion of freedom in the absolute sense in which it was used is included in this rediscovery. This is not determinism. Existentialism is certainly not determinism. But existentialism and especially psychoanalysis and the whole philosophy of the unconscious have rediscovered the totality of the personality in which not only the conscious elements are decisive.

The fourth point, connected with the previous one, is that moralism can be conquered to a great extent in Christian theology. The call for moralism was one of the great forms of self-estrangement of theology from its whole being. And it is indeed important to know that theology had to learn from the psychoanalytic method the meaning of grace, the meaning of forgiveness as acceptance of those who are unacceptable and not of those who are the good people. On the contrary, the non-good people are those who are accepted, or in religious language, forgiven, justified, whatever you wish to call it. The word grace, which had lost any meaning, has gained a new meaning by the way in which the analyst deals with his patient. He accepts him. He does not say, "You are acceptable," but he accepts him. And that is the way in which, according to religious symbolism, God deals with us; and it is the way every minister and every Christian should deal with the other person.

Before the rediscovery of confession and counselling (which were completely lost in Protestantism), everybody was asked to do something, and if he didn't do it he was reproached. Now he can go to somebody, can talk to him, and in talking he can objectify what is in him and get rid of it.

If the counsellor or confessor is somebody who knows the human situation, he can be a medium of grace for him who comes to him, a medium for the feeling of overcoming the cleavage between essence and existence.

Finally, what is the influence of psychoanalysis on systematic theology? The interpretation of man's predicament by psychoanalysis raises the question that is implied in man's very existence. Systematic theology has to show that the religious symbols are answers to this question. Now, if you understand the relation of theology and depth psychology in this way, you have grasped the fundamental importance, the final and decisive importance, of all this for theology. There is no theistic and non-theistic existentialism or psychoanalysis. They analyze the human situation. Whenever the analysts or the philosophers give an answer, they do it not as existentialists. They do it from other traditions, whether it be Catholic, Protestant, Lutheran, humanist, or socialist. Traditions come from everywhere, but they do not come from the *question*.

In a long talk in London with T. S. Eliot, who is really considered to be an existentialist, we talked about just this problem. I told him, "I believe that you cannot answer the question you develop in your plays and your poems on the basis of your plays and poems, because they only develop the question—they describe human existence. But if there is an answer, it comes from somewhere else." He replied, "That is exactly what I am fighting for all the time. I am, as you know, an Episcopalian." And he is really a faithful Episcopalian; he answers as an Episcopalian but not as an existentialist. This means that the existentialist raises the question and analyzes the human situation to which the theologian can then give the answer, an answer given not from the question but from somewhere else, and not from the human situation itself.

Theology has received tremendous gifts from existentialism and psychoanalysis, gifts not dreamed of fifty years ago or even thirty years ago. We have these gifts. Existentialists and analysts themselves do not need to know that they have given to theology these great things. But the theologians should know it.

IX

Science and Theology:
A Discussion with Einstein

SEVERAL years ago Albert Einstein delivered an address on "Science and Religion," which aroused considerable opposition among religious people and theologians because of his rejection of the idea of the Personal God.* If it had not been Einstein, the great transformer of our physical world view, his arguments probably would not have produced any excitement, for they were neither new nor powerful in themselves. But in the mouth of Einstein, as an expression of his intellectual and moral character, they became significant. Therefore it is justified that philosophical or apologetic theology not only deals with Einstein's criticism but tries to sketch a solution in which this criticism is accepted and overcome at the same time.

Einstein attacked the idea of a Personal God from four angles: The idea is not essential for religion. It is the creation of primitive superstition. It is self-contradictory. It contradicts the scientific world view.

The first argument presupposes a definition of the nature of religion leaving out everything in which religion differs from ethics: Religion is the acceptance of and devotion to

* Dr. Einstein's paper was one of a number prepared for the sessions of the conference on "Science, Philosophy, and Religion" held on September 9, 10, and 11, 1940, in New York City.

superpersonal values. But the question whether this is an adequate definition of religion cannot be answered before the question is answered whether the idea of the Personal God has some objective meaning or not. Therefore we must turn to the second argument, the historical.

It does not show and cannot show why primitive imagination created just the idea of *God*. There is no doubt that this idea has been used and abused by all kinds of superstition and immorality. But in order to be abused it first must have been used. Its abuse does not tell anything about its genesis. Looking at the tremendous impact the idea of God always has made on human thought and behavior, the theory that all this was a product of an uneducated arbitrary imagination appears utterly inadequate. Mythological phantasy can create stories about gods, but it cannot create the idea of God itself, because the idea transcends all the elements of experience which constitute mythology. As Descartes argues: the infinite in our mind presupposes the infinite itself.

The third argument of Einstein challenges the idea of an omnipotent God who creates moral and physical evil although, on the other hand, he is supposed to be good and righteous. This criticism presupposes a concept of omnipotence which identifies omnipotence with omni-activity in terms of physical causality. But it is an old, and always emphasized, theological doctrine that God acts in all beings according to their special nature; in man according to his rational nature, in animals and plants according to their organic nature, in stones according to their inorganic nature. The symbol of omnipotence expresses the religious experience that no structure of reality and no event in nature and history has the power of removing us from community with the infinite and inexhaustible ground of meaning and being. What "omnipotence" means should be found in the words Deutero-Isaiah (Is. 40) speaks to the exiled in Babylon when he describes the nothingness of the world-empires in comparison with the divine power to fulfill its historical aim through an infinitely small group of exiled people. Or what "omnipotence" means can be found in the words Paul (Rom. 8) speaks to the few Christians in the slums of the big cities when he pronounces that neither natural nor political powers, neither earthly nor heavenly forces can separate us from the "Love of God." If the idea of omnipotence is taken out of this context and transformed into the description of a special form of causality, it becomes not only self-contradicting—as Einstein rightly states—but also absurd and irreligious.

This leads to the last and most important argument of Einstein: The idea of a Personal God contradicts the scientific interpretation of nature. Before dealing with this argument, we should make two methodological remarks: Firstly we can agree entirely with Einstein when he warns the theologians not to build their doctrines in the dark spots of scientific research. This was the bad method of some apologetic fanatics of nineteenth-century theology, but it never was the attitude of any great theologian. Theology, above all, must leave to science the description of the whole of objects and their interdependence in nature and history, in man and his world. And beyond this, theology must leave to philosophy the description of the structures and categories of being itself and of the *logos* in which being becomes manifest. Any interference of theology with these tasks of philosophy and science is destructive for theology itself.

Secondly we must ask every critic of theology to deal with theology with the same fairness which is demanded from everyone who deals, for instance, with physics—namely, to attack the most advanced and not some obsolete forms of a discipline. After Schleiermacher and Hegel had received

Spinoza's doctrine of God as an intrinsic element of any theological doctrine of God, just as the early theologians, Origen and Augustine, had received Plato's idea of God as an inherent element in their doctrine of God, it became impossible to use the most primitive pattern of the concept of the Personal God in order to challenge the idea itself. The concept of a "Personal God," interfering with natural events, or being "an independent cause of natural events," makes God a natural object beside others, an object among objects, a being among beings, maybe the highest, but nevertheless *a* being. This, indeed, is the destruction, not only of the physical system, but even more the destruction of any meaningful idea of God. It is the impure mixture of mythological elements (which are justified in their place, namely, in the concrete religious life) and of rational elements (which are justified in their place, namely, in the theological interpretation of religious experience). No criticism of this distorted idea of God can be sharp enough.

In order to indicate an idea of the Personal God, which by no means can interfere with science or philosophy as such, we can turn to some beautiful words of Einstein: the true scientist "attains that humble attitude of mind towards the grandeur of reason incarnate in existence, which, in its profoundest depths, is inaccessible to man." If we interpret these words rightly, they point to a common ground of the whole of the physical world and of suprapersonal values; a ground which, on the one hand, is manifest in the structure of being (the physical world) and meaning (the good, true, and beautiful), and which, on the other hand, is hidden in its inexhaustible depth.

Now this is the first and basic element of any developed idea of God from the earliest Greek philosophers to present-day theology. The manifestation of this ground and abyss of being and meaning creates what modern theology calls "the experience of the numinous." Such an experience can occur in connection with the intuition of the "grandeur of reason incarnate in existence"; it can occur in connection with the belief in "the significance and loftiness of those suprapersonal objects and goals which neither require nor are capable of rational foundation," as Einstein says. The same experience can occur, and occurs for the large majority of men, in connection with the impression some persons, historical or natural events, objects, words, pictures, tunes, dreams, etc. make on the human soul, creating the feeling of the holy, that is, of the presence of the "numinous." In such experiences religion lives and tries to maintain the presence of, and community with, this divine depth of our existence. But since it is "inaccessible" to any objectifying concept it must be expressed in symbols.

One of these symbols is Personal God. It is the common opinion of classical theology, in practically all periods of Church history, that the predicate "personal" can be said of the Divine only symbolically or by analogy or if affirmed and negated at the same time. It is obvious that in the daily life of religion the symbolic character of the idea of the Personal God is not always realized. This is dangerous only if distorting theoretical or practical consequences are derived from the failure to realize it. Then attacks from outside and criticism from inside follow and must follow. They are demanded by religion itself. Without an element of "atheism" no "theism" can be maintained.

But why must the symbol of the personal be used at all? The answer can be given through a term used by Einstein himself: the supra-personal. The depth of being cannot be symbolized by objects taken from a realm which is lower than the personal, from the realm of things or sub-personal living beings. The supra-personal is not an "It," or more exactly, it is a "He" as much as it is an "It," and it is above both of them. But if the "He" element is left out, the "It" element transforms the alleged supra-personal into a sub-personal, as usually happens in monism and pantheism. And such a neutral sub-personal cannot grasp the center of our personality; it can satisfy our aesthetic feeling or our intellectual needs, but it cannot convert our will, it cannot overcome our loneliness, anxiety, and despair. For as the philosopher Schelling says: "Only a person can heal a person." This is the reason that the symbol of the Personal God is indispensable for living religion. It is a symbol, not an object, and it never should be interpreted as an object. And it is one symbol beside others indicating that our personal center is grasped by the manifestation of the inaccessible ground and abyss of being.

X

Moralisms and Morality: Theonomous Ethics

THE title of this chapter requires a few "semantic" considerations, for neither the word "moralisms" nor the word "morality" is unambiguous. "Moralism" designates an attitude toward life, an attitude which is widespread in this country. It is the distortion of the moral imperative into an oppressive law. One can find a puritan, an evangelistic, a nationalistic, and simply a conventional moralism (which is not conscious of its historical roots). Moralism as the distortion of the moral imperative has no plural. It is an attitude, a negative one, against which theology and psychology should wage a common war.

"Moralisms" (in plural) does not mean something negative. It points to systems of moral imperatives as they have developed in special cultures and are dependent upon the relativities and limitations of these cultures. There is, however, an essential relation between the meaning of the plural and the singular of moralism: Moral systems, just because of their intimate connection with a cultural system, have the tendency to become oppressive if the general cultural scheme changes. They tend to produce moralism as an attitude. The distinction between moralisms as ethical systems and moralism as a negative attitude is identical with the distinction between the creative and the oppressive character of moral imperatives, and each ethical system has both characteristics.

The other term to be considered is morality. It is as ambiguous as the term moralism. Morality, in the first place, is the experience of the moral imperative. It is a function of man as man. Without it he would not be man. A being without the consciousness of a moral demand is not human. If a feeble-minded child behaves as if he were unaware of any moral demand, he is sub-human, which does not mean that he is an animal. He is both more and less than an animal. In contrast to him, a criminal is aware of the moral imperative, while defying its commands. He is human although he fights against an essential element in human nature. For man as man has the potentiality to contradict himself.

Morality can also mean "moral behavior," the attempt to be obedient to a system of moral rules. The contrast to morality in this sense should be immorality (in difference to the amorality of subhuman beings). But unfortunately the word "immoral" can hardly be used since, through the special Anglo-Saxon moralism, it has received an almost exclusively sexual connotation. Immorality in the general sense of anti-moral behavior is possible only in a limited way. Even the criminal shows morality, although he follows a moralistic code which contradicts the accepted moralism of a society.

After this attempt at semantic clarification, there are now four central questions which this chapter should raise under the following four headings:

I. Moralisms Conditioned, Morality Unconditional

II. Moralisms of Authority and Morality of Risk

III. Moralisms of Law and Morality of Grace

IV. Moralisms of Justice and Morality of Love

I. MORALISMS CONDITIONED, MORALITY UNCONDITIONAL

People today are afraid of the term "unconditional." This is understandable if one considers the way in which many rather conditioned ideas and methods have been imposed on individuals and groups in the name of an unconditional truth, authoritatively and through suppression. The destructive consequences of such a demonic absolutism have produced a reaction even against the term unconditional. The mere word provokes passionate resistance. But not everything which is psychologically understandable is for this reason true. Even the most outspoken relativists cannot avoid something absolute. They acknowledge the unconditional quest to follow logical rules in their reasoning, and to act according to the law of scientific honesty in their thinking and speaking. Their character as scientific personalities is dependent on the unconditional acceptance of these principles.

This leads us to a more general understanding of the unconditional character of the moral imperative. What Immanuel Kant has called the "categorical imperative" is nothing more than the unconditional character of the "ought-to-be," the moral commandment. Whatever its content may be, its form is unconditional. One can rightly criticize Kant because he establishes a system of ethical forms without ethical contents. But just this limitation is his greatness. It makes as sharp as possible the distinction between morality which is unconditional, and moralisms which are valid only conditionally and within limits. If this is understood, the relativity of all concrete ethics (moralisms) is accepted and emphasized. The material cited by the sociologist, anthropologist, and psychologist showing the endless differences of ethical ideals is no argument against the unconditional validity of the moral imperative. If we disregard this distinction, we either fall into an absolute skepticism which, in the long run, undermines morality as such, or we fall into an absolutism which attributes unconditional validity to one of the many possible moralisms. Since, however, each of these moralisms has to maintain itself against others, it becomes fanatical, for fanaticism is the attempt to repress elements of one's own being for the sake of others. If the fanatic encounters these elements in somebody else, he fights against them passionately, because they endanger the success of his own repression.

The reason for the unconditional character of the moral imperative is that it puts our essential being as a demand against us. The moral imperative is not a strange law, imposed on us, but it is the law of our own being. In the moral imperative we ourselves, in our essential being, are put against ourselves, in our actual being. No outside command can be unconditional, whether it comes from a state, or a person, or God—if God is thought of as an outside power, establishing a law for our behavior. A stranger, even if his name were God, who imposes commands upon us must be resisted or, as Nietzsche has expressed it in his symbol of the "ugliest man," he must be killed because nobody can stand him. We cannot be obedient to the commands of a stranger even if he is God. Nor can we take unconditionally the content of the moral imperative from human authorities like traditions, conventions, political or religious authorities. There is no ultimate authority in them. One is largely dependent on them, but none of them is unconditionally valid.

The moral command is unconditional because it is we ourselves commanding ourselves. Morality is the self-affirmation of our essential being. This makes it unconditional, whatever its content may be. This is quite different from an affirmation of one's self in terms of one's desires and fears.

Such a self-affirmation has no unconditional character; ethics based on it are ethics of calculation, describing the best way of getting fulfillment of desires and protection against fears. There is nothing absolute in technical calculation. But morality as the self-affirmation of one's essential being is unconditional.

The contents, however, of the moral self-affirmation are conditioned, relative, dependent on the social and psychological constellation. While morality as the pure form of essential self-affirmation is absolute, the concrete systems of moral imperatives, the "moralisms" are relative. This is not relativism (which as a philosophical attitude is self-contradictory), but it is the acknowledgment of man's finitude and his dependence on the contingencies of time and space. No conflict between the ethicist, theological or philosophical, and the anthropologist or sociologist is necessary. No theologian should deny the relativity of the moral contents; no ethnologist should deny the absolute character of the ethical demand.

Against the doctrine of the relativity of moral contents, the concept of "natural law" seems to stand. But it is only in the Roman Catholic interpretation of the moral law that a conflict exists. Natural, according to classical doctrine, is the law which is implied in man's essential nature. It has been given in creation, it has been lost by "the fall," it has been restated by Moses and Jesus (there is no difference between natural and revealed law in Bible and classical theology). The restatement of the natural law was, at the same time, its formalization and its concentration into one all-embracing law, the "Great Commandment," the commandment of love.

There is, however, a difference between the Protestant and the Catholic doctrine of the natural law. Catholicism believes that the natural law has definite contents, which are unchangeable and are authoritatively stated by the Church (e.g. the fight of the Roman Church against birth control). Protestantism, on the other hand, at least today and in this country, determines the contents of the natural law largely by ethical traditions and conventions; but this is done without a supporting theory, and therefore Protestantism has the possibility of a dynamic concept of natural law. It can protest against each moral content which claims unconditional character. This whole chapter is an attempt to protest, in the name of the Protestant principle, against the Protestant moralism as it has developed in Protestant countries.

II. MORALISMS OF AUTHORITY AND MORALITY OF RISK

Systems of ethical rules, that is moralisms, are imposed on the masses by authorities: religious authorities as the Roman Church, quasi-religious authorities as the totalitarian governments, secular authorities as the givers of positive laws, conventional, family, and school authorities. "Imposing" in a radical sense means forming a conscience. External imposition is not sufficient for the creation of a moral system. It must be internalized. Only a system which is internalized is safe. Only commands which have become natural will be obeyed in extreme situations. The obedience is complete if it works automatically.

Conscience has been interpreted in different ways. The concept of internalization points to the fact that even conscience is not above the relativity which characterizes all ethical contents. It is neither the infallible voice of God, nor the infallible awareness of the natural law. It is, as the German philosopher Heidegger has said, the call, often the silent call, of man to be himself. But the self to which the conscience calls is the essential, not as Heidegger believes, the existential self. It calls us to what we essentially are, but it does not tell with certainty what that is. Even the conscience can judge us erroneously. It does not help us to a valid moral decision if one says with many theologians and philosophers: Always follow your conscience. This does not say, for example, what to do if the conscience is split. As long as the conscience points unambiguously in one direction, it is comparatively safe to follow it. Split authority destroys authority, in human relations, as well as in one's conscience.

Authority has a double meaning and a double function in the context of our problem. One is born into a moral universe, produced by the experience of all former generations. It is a mixture of natural interest, especially of the ruling classes, and wisdom, acquired by the leading people. A moral universe is not only an ideology, that is, a product of the will to gain and to preserve power. It is also a result of experience and real wisdom. It gives the material in which moral decisions are made. And every single decision adds to the experience and the wisdom of the whole. In this sense, we all are dependent on authority, on factual authority, or, as Erich Fromm has called it, rational authority. Everyone has, in some realm, rational authority above the others. For everyone contributes in a unique way to the life of the whole. And his unique experience gives, even to the least educated man, some authority over the highest educated one.

But besides this factual authority which is mutual and exercised by everybody, there is the established authority which is one-sided and exercised by selected individuals or groups. If they represent the ethical realm, they participate in the unconditional character of the moral imperative. These authorities gain absolute authority because of the absolute character of what they stand for. This analysis contradicts the way in which the idea of God is derived by some philosophers and psychologists from the unconditional impact of the father image on the child. One calls God the projection of the father image. But every projection is not only a projection *of* something, but it is also a projection *upon* something. What is this "something" upon which the image of the father is "projected" so that it becomes divine? The answer can only be: It is projected upon the "screen" of the unconditional! And this screen is not projected. It makes projection possible. So we do not reject the theory of projection (which is as old as philosophical thought), but we try to refine it. It has to be constructed in three steps. The first and basic step is the assertion that man, as man, experiences something unconditional in terms of the unconditional character of the moral imperative.

The second step is the recognition that the early dependence on the father, or on father figures, drives to a projection of the father image upon the screen of the unconditional.

The third step is the insight that this identification of the concrete media of the unconditional with the unconditional itself is, religiously speaking, demonic, psychologically speaking, neurotic. Education and psychotherapy can and must dissolve this kind of father image, but they cannot dissolve the element of the unconditional itself, for this is essentially human.

Since the ethical authorities are not absolute (in spite of the absolute character of the moral imperative), every moral act includes a risk. The human situation itself is such a risk. In order to become human, man must trespass the "state of innocence," but when he has trespassed it he finds himself in a state of self-contradiction. This situation, which is a permanent one, is symbolized in the story of the Paradise. Man must always trespass the safety regions which are circumscribed by ethical authorities. He must enter the spheres of unsafety and uncertainty. A morality which plays safe, by subjecting itself to an unconditional authority, is suspect. It has not the courage to take guilt and tragedy upon itself. True morality is a morality of risk. It is a morality which is based on the "courage to be," the dynamic self-affirmation of man as man. This self-affirmation must take the threat of non-being, death, guilt, and meaninglessness into itself. It risks itself, and through the courage of risking itself, it wins itself. Moralisms give safety, morality lives in the unsafety of risk and courage.

III. MORALISMS OF LAW AND MORALITY OF GRACE

Because the moral imperative puts our essential against our actual being, it appears to us as law. A being which lives out of its essential nature is law to itself. It follows its natural structure. But this is not the human situation. Man is estranged from his essential being and, therefore, the moral imperative appears as law to him: Moralism is legalism!

The law is first of all "natural law." In the Stoic tradition this term does not mean the physical laws but the natural laws which constitute our essential nature. These laws are the background of all positive laws in states and other groups. They are also the background of the moral law, which is our problem today. The moral law is more oppressive than the severest positive law, just because it is internalized. It creates conscience and the feeling of guilt.

So we must ask: What is the power inducing us to fulfill the law? The power behind the positive laws is rewards and punishments. What is the power behind the moral law? One could say: the reward of the good and the punishment of the uneasy conscience, often projected as heavenly rewards and punishments in purgatory or hell. (Cf. Hamlet's words about the conscience, which makes cowards of us.) But this answer is not sufficient. It does not explain the insuperable resistance the law provokes against itself, in spite of punishments and rewards. The law is not able to create its own fulfillment.

The reason for this is visible when we consider the words of Jesus, Paul, and Luther saying that the law is only fulfilled if it is fulfilled with joy, and not with resentment and hate. But joy cannot be commanded. The law brings us into a paradoxical situation: It commands, which means that it stands against us. But it commands something which can be done only if it does *not* stand against us, if we are united with what it commands. This is the point where the moral imperative drives towards something which is not command but reality. Only the "good tree" brings "good fruits." Only if being precedes that which ought-to-be, can the ought-to-be be fulfilled. Morality can be maintained only through that which is given and not through that which is demanded; in religious terms, through grace and not through law. Without the re-union of man with his own essential nature no perfect moral act is possible. Legalism drives either to self-complacency (I have kept *all* commandments) or to despair (I cannot keep *any* commandment). Moralism of law makes pharisees or cynics, or it produces in the majority of people an indifference which lowers the moral imperative to conventional behavior. Moralism necessarily ends in the quest for grace.

Grace unites two elements: the overcoming of guilt and the overcoming of estrangement. The first element appears in theology as the "forgiveness of sins," or in more recent terminology, as "accepting acceptance though being unacceptable." The second element appears in theology as "regeneration" or in more recent terminology, as the "entering into the new being" which is above the split between what we are and what we ought to be. Every religion, even if seemingly moralistic, has a doctrine of salvation in which these two elements are present.

And psychotherapy is involved in the same problems. Psychotherapy is definitely antimoralistic. It avoids commandments because it knows that neurotics cannot be healed by moral judgments and moral demands. The only help is to accept him who is unacceptable, to create a communion with him, a sphere of participation in a new reality. Psychotherapy must be a therapy of grace or it cannot be therapy at all. There are striking analogies between the recent methods of mental healing and the traditional ways of personal salvation. But there is also one basic difference. Psychotherapy can liberate one from a special difficulty. Religion shows to him who is liberated, and has to decide about the meaning and aim of his existence, a final way. This difference is decisive for the independence as well as for the co-operation of religion and psychotherapy.

IV. MORALISMS OF JUSTICE AND MORALITY OF LOVE

The moral imperative expresses itself in laws which are supposed to be just. Justice, in Greek thinking, is the unity of the whole system of morals. Justice, in the Old Testament, is that quality of God which makes Him the Lord of the Universe. In Islam, morality and law are not distinguished, and in the philosophy of Hegel, ethics are treated as a section of the philosophy of law (*Recht*). Every system of moral commandments is, at the same time, the basis for a system of laws. In all moralisms the moral imperative has the tendency to become a legal principle. Justice, in Aristotle, is determined by proportionality. Everybody gets what he deserves according to quantitative measurements. This is not the Christian point of view. Justice, in the Old Testament, is the activity of God toward the fulfillment of His promises. And justice, in the New Testament, is the unity of judgment and forgiveness. Justification by grace is the highest form of divine justice. This means that proportional justice is not the answer to the moral problem. Not proportional, but transforming justice has divine character. In other words: Justice is fulfilled in love. The moralisms of justice drive toward the morality of love.

Love, in the sense of this statement, is not an emotion, but a principle of life. If love were primarily emotion it would inescapably conflict with justice, it would add something to justice which is not justice. But love does not add something strange to justice. Rather it is the ground, the power, and the aim of justice. Love is the life which separates itself from itself and drives toward reunion with itself. The norm of justice is reunion of the estranged. Creative justice—justice, creative as love—is the union of love and justice and the ultimate principle of morality.

From this it follows that there is a just self-love, namely the desire of reunion of oneself with oneself. One can be loveless toward oneself. But if this is the case, one is not only without love but also without justice toward oneself—and toward others. One must accept oneself just as one is accepted in spite of being unacceptable. And in doing so one has what is called the right self-love, the opposite of the wrong self-love. In order to avoid many confusions one should replace the word self-love completely. One may call the right self-love self-acceptance, the wrong self-love selfishness, and the natural self-love self-affirmation. In all cases the word "self," as such, has no negative connotations. It is the structure of the most developed form of reality, the most individualized and the most universal being. Self is good, self-affirmation is good, self-acceptance is good, but selfishness is bad because it prevents both self-affirmation and self-acceptance.

Love is the answer to the problem of moralisms and morality. It answers the questions implied in all four confrontations of moralism and morality. Love is unconditional. There is nothing which could condition it by a higher principle. There is nothing above love. And love conditions itself. It enters every concrete situation and works for the reunion of the separated in a unique way.

Love transforms the moralisms of authority into a morality of risk. Love is creative and creativity includes risk. Love does not destroy factual authority but it liberates from the authority of a special place, from an irrational hypostatized authority. Love participates, and participation overcomes authority.

Love is the source of grace. Love accepts that which is unacceptable and love renews the old being so that it becomes a new being. Medieval theology almost identified love and grace, and rightly so, for that which makes one graceful is love. But grace is, at the same time, the love which forgives and accepts.

Nevertheless, love includes justice. Love without justice is a body without a backbone. The justice of love includes that no partner in this relation is asked to annihilate himself. The self which enters a love relation is preserved in its independence. Love includes justice to others and to oneself. Love is the solution of the problem: moralisms and morality.

XI

A Theology of Education

I. EDUCATIONAL AIMS AND THEIR RELATIONS

ONE can distinguish three educational aims, the technical education, the humanistic education, the inducting education. Modern liberal education combines elements of technical with elements of humanistic education. In the Middle Ages, up to the century of the Reformation, technical education was combined with inducting education. The revolutionary movements of the 20th century tried to return to the medieval combination of technical with inducting education. Among the three, technical education, namely the education for skills, special ones like crafts and arts, and general ones like reading, writing, and arithmetic, has existed as long as human beings have taught their children how to use tools skillfully. Yet it was always more than mere technical education. It included many elements of the humanistic way: discipline, subjection to the demands of the object in knowing and handling it, participation in the community of work, subordination to and criticism of the demands of the expert and of the community. All these are elements which belong to the humanistic aim of education, but the humanistic ideal itself goes far beyond them. It can be described as the ideal of the development of all human potentialities, individually and socially. It is both the discovery and the creation of the philosophers and artists of the Renaissance, and it has determined, whether accepted or rejected, the educational history of the last four centuries. Its roots lie not in human arrogance, as theological polemics often contended, but rather in the basic religious experience of the early Renaissance, namely, the presence of the infinite in everything finite. Every human being, they felt, is a microcosm, a small universe in whom the large universe is mirrored. As a mirror of the universe and its divine ground, the individual is unique, incomparable, infinitely significant, able to develop in freedom his given endowment. Education is supposed to actualize his potentialities, generally and individually. The aim of the educational process is the humanistic personality in whom as many potentialities as possible are developed, among them being technical skills and the religious function.

The humanistic ideal of education has arisen in contrast to the inducting education, of which the medieval culture provides the most important example, important at least for the Western world. Elements of inducting education were never totally absent. The induction of children into their families, with the tradition, symbols, and demands of the family, is the basic form of inducting education. Its aim is not development of the potentialities of the individual, but induction into the actuality of a group, the life and spirit of community, family, tribe, town, nation, church. Such an induction happens spontaneously through the participation of the individual in the life of the group. But it can also be made a matter of intellectual guidance. The form in which this happens is the interpretation of the institutions and symbols of the group in which the child or the new adult member already lives. Induction precedes interpretation, but interpretation makes the induction complete. One of the best examples is the way in which the Old Testament commands parents to tell the story of the exodus from Egypt, if the children inquire about the meaning of the festival in which they already participate. The recent demand for more American history in the schools has not humanistic but inducting educational reasons. The life and the symbols of the nation, their past and their traditions, shall be interpreted to those who already participate in them, but who are not yet conscious of their meaning.

It is obvious that the Church School belongs predominantly, though not exclusively, to the inducting type of educational ideas.

But our next question must be, how did the three educational ideas develop in relation to each other and within themselves, and what is their present situation? This question could be fully answered only by a complete history of modern educational ideas. A short summary of the decisive developments must replace it. One could say that each of the three ideas tried more or less successfully to subject the others to itself. In the beginning of the modern period, inducting education was in almost uncontested power. The reality into which generation after generation were inducted was the Christian Church, or more precisely, the *"corpus Christianum,"* the "body Christian," which embraced religion, politics, and culture. The soul of this body, namely, the spirit of medieval Christianity, was present and exercised educational functions on every level of man's individual and social life. Even the education for skills was permeated by the religious-cultural substance of the Christian body. Elements of humanistic education were used only for the interpretation of the substance, its symbols and traditions, in order to train the representatives and leaders of the whole body.

When the humanistic ideal of education revolted against the power of the inducting education, a development started which still largely determines our own spiritual destiny. In the beginning the humanistic education was outspokenly aristocratic. All human potentialities should be developed in the outstanding individual, belonging to the old feudal or the new high bourgeois classes. For the others the training in basic and specialist skills became more and more urgent and was partly done by the foundation of public schools. The inducting element in these schools was the induction into the morals and beliefs of the bourgeois society. Remnants of the old inducting education were the Church Schools, which however had to adapt themselves to the demands for an enlarged technical and an intensified humanistic education. During the 19th century, the technical ideal of education subjected the humanistic ideal largely to itself. Humanism became empty, deprived of creative content. The cultural creations of the past were, and are, used as a means for education, but without a focus and a spiritual center. They became goods, the possession of which distinguished the upper classes of society, as material goods did.

In this way, the technical aim of education became predominant. Adjustment to the demands of the industrial society became the main educational purpose. The cultural heritage and the religious institutions were not rejected but subjected to this purpose. Yet the industrial society is divided into national units. Therefore, the adjustment to the demands of industrial society became the demand to adjust oneself to a national group within the industrial society. In this way, the emptiness of the late humanistic education was covered up by the national idea. Education to good citizenship seemed to combine all three educational aims: induction into the spirit of the nation and its institutions, training in general and special skills, and mediation of the cultural goods of past and present. The programs of most schools and the proclamations of most school boards and educational conferences confirm daily the effectiveness of this ideal. How can the Church School stand beside or against its overwhelming influence?

No matter how we answer this question, the educational idea of our present society in this and other Western countries shows heavy problems and deep inner conflicts. Certainly it serves well the aim of inducting the new generations into the demands of the monstrous process of mass production and mass consumption which characterizes our industrial society as a whole, in spite of its national divisions. The new generation receives the general skills in a high perfection; it is being trained in the special skills, partly by vocational schools, but mostly by participation in the different crafts, arts, and professions themselves. And more than this, there is a large amount of psychological adjustment to the needs of the industrial society in most members of the younger generation. The way in this country—in contrast to the way in Europe—is a kind of permissiveness which makes it possible for young people to express their willfulness and aggressiveness uninhibited by a stern discipline, but in such a way that after several years an astonishing adjustment to the demands of contemporary society has taken place and the revolutionary spirit of the young has evaporated. They have become, almost overnight, good citizens, able to fill a position in our competitive society, receptive of cultural goods, especially if they enjoyed a college education with millions of others.

The questions, however, must be whether the induction into a national section of the industrial society fulfills the ideal of induction, and whether the mediation of cultural goods fulfills the ideal of humanistic development. Both questions provoke a negative answer. The ideal of induction as actualized in the medieval society, transcended social and national boundaries. They were not absent, but the ultimate aim of education went beyond them to something ultimate, unconditional, universal. The induction of the Middle Ages was induction into a community with symbols in which the answers to the questions of human existence and its meaning were embodied. One can say that *induction was initiation into the mystery of human existence.*

This was still the situation long after the Middle Ages in countries or sections of countries in which the churches, Catholic or Protestant, determined the spirit of education. The public school in eastern Germany around the turn of this century was, in all of its procedures, an institution to initiate the young into the Christian-Lutheran answer to the questions of existence. The national element was strong but not decisive. In the secondary school, the national element prevailed over the religious, and at the universities neither the one nor the other was effective. In this country, the public school has ceased to give an education which in any sense could be called initiation into the mystery of existence and the symbols through which it is expressed. The national ideal can in no way replace an induction which is initiation. This is the point on which the question of the Church-determined school must be raised.

But another unsolved problem of contemporary education must be brought out, namely, its claim to be humanistic. It considers the human potentialities as expressions of man's being a mirror of the universe and its creative ground. When the religious substance of humanism disappeared, the mere form was left, abundant, but empty. And today the means of mass communication mediate these empty remnants of former cultural creations to everybody day and night. But we must ask: which of these cultural goods speaks to us as the German poet Rilke felt that the torso of a Greek Apollo spoke to him—"Change thy life!"? Cultural goods have become trimmings, means for having a good time, but nothing ultimately serious, nothing through which the mystery of being grasps us. Humanism has become empty, and so has the humanistic ideal of education.

It is not surprising that this double emptiness, the emptiness of adjustment to the demands of the industrial society, and the emptiness of cultural goods without ultimate seriousness, lead to indifference, cynicism, despair, mental disturbances, early crimes, disgust of life. Neither is it surprising that, in reaction to this emptiness, forces arose which tried to re-establish systems of life and thought which give meaning and spiritual security and which make inducting education toward a meaningful life possible. This refers to the resurgence of ecclesiastical authority both in the Catholic and in the Protestant Church.

One could observe how the European youth before the Second World War were longing for symbols in which they could see a convincing expression of the meaning of existence. They desired to be initiated into these symbols which demanded unconditional surrender, even if they showed very soon their demonic-destructive character. The young ones wanted something *absolutely serious*—in contrast to the playing with cultural goods. They wanted something for which they could sacrifice themselves, even if it was a distorted religious-political aim. From here the place of the Church School in the spiritual geography of our time can be determined. It is a place where the medieval tradition of inductive education is still alive (although the demands of technical education into the structure of our industrial society are acknowledged). But the problem of humanistic education is still unsolved in the Church Schools. The remaining part of this chapter will be devoted to a consideration of this problem.

II. THE INDUCTING AND THE HUMANIST
ELEMENT IN THE CHURCH SCHOOL

In contrast to the medieval situation, the contemporary Church School—and church-directed school—is dependent on a small section of the religious life, a special denomination or a special confessional group. It does not represent the spirit of our society as a whole. It is not an expression of its substance, its soul. Therefore, its life, like the life of a theological seminary, can fall into a state of isolation, of concentration on itself, its tradition and symbols. The induction into these symbols and traditions would be ideally an induction of the character of an initiation, but on too small a basis, and therefore not strong enough to give a personal center which can radiate into all sectors of contemporary life.

There is another problem: the pupil who is inducted into the reality and the symbols of a special denomination or confession through the community of the school (which in most cases is a continuation of the community of the family) normally comes to a point at which he doubts, or turns away from, or attacks the reality and the symbols into which he has been inducted. Living in a world hardly touched by the traditions which have come to him, he inescapably becomes skeptical, both from a religious and from a cultural point of view. And if the invisible power of the spirit of his school was very strong, his reaction against it will be equally strong. Is there a way to overcome these dangers of the Church School?

In order to answer this question, we must ask about the relation of the ideal of inducting education, which underlies the life of the Church School, to the ideal of humanistic education, which is actualized in the Church School only in a limited way. Development of potentialities, not induction into a set of practical and theoretical symbols, is the meaning of humanistic education. This seems to produce an insoluble conflict. But there is a solution, and it is just the inner conflicts of the Church School itself which point to the solution of the conflict between inducting and humanistic education.

Religious induction faces two main difficulties: one is the fact that it has to give answers to questions which never have been asked by the child. In speaking of God and the Christ and the Church, or of sin and salvation and the kingdom of God, religious education mediates a material which cannot be received by the mind of those who have not asked the questions to which these words give answers. These words are like stones, thrown at them, from which sooner or later they must turn away. Therefore, every religious educator must try to find the existentially important questions which are alive in the minds and hearts of the pupils. It must make the pupil aware of the questions which he already has.

After this has been done, he can be shown that the traditional symbols in myth and cult originally were conceived as answers to the questions implied in man's very existence. The correlation of question and answer gives meaning to the answers and opens up the mind of the pupil to the symbols into which religious education has inducted him. But where questions are asked or provoked and the answers are interpreted in the light of the question, there the humanistic spirit is at work. For humanism starts with the most radical question, the question of being—of being generally and of my own being particularly. The humanistic question is radical; it goes to the roots and does not accept anything whatsoever as being beyond questioning.

One has often thought that this is the opposite of religious faith, which has been described as an unquestionable certainty in which all asking comes to rest. Indeed, there are interpretations of faith which make faith a castle surrounded by walls of authority which doubt cannot pierce. But this is certainly not the biblical or the Protestant concept of faith. In every act of faith, there is risk, and the courage to take this risk, and the necessary doubt which distinguishes faith from mathematical or empirical evidence. Faith, and the radical question with which humanism starts, do not contradict each other if faith is seen as comprising itself and the doubt about itself. The Church School, on its way of inducting pupils into the symbols and realities of the Christian life, must remain aware of the fact that Christianity has accepted the humanistic principle by identifying Jesus as the Christ with the universal Logos, the creative structure of everything that is. Christianity includes humanism and the radical question of truth which is the first principle of humanism. The inducting education of the Church School can and must include the principle of humanist education, the correlation between question and answer, the radicalism of the question, the opening up of all human possibilities, and the providing of opportunities where the pupil may develop in freedom.

The second problem of the Church School which helps to answer the question of the relationship between the inducting and the humanistic aim of education is based on the symbolic character of religious language and the mythical form of all religious propositions. The great art of the religious educator is to transform the primitive literalism with respect to the religious symbols into a conceptual interpretation without destroying the power of the symbols. Many despair of such a possibility. They either refuse to help the pupil in this necessary transformation or they refuse to give him the traditional symbols before he is able to interpret them conceptually. Both ways are wrong. If you do not impress the religious symbols on the receptive minds of young children, they will experience the full power of the religious symbols only in the rare event of a late conversion. One should not allow a religiously empty space in children up to the moment in which they can fully understand the meaning of the symbols. Nobody can say exactly how much or how little a young child takes from a ritual act into his unconsciousness, even if he understands almost nothing of it. Here the Church School and its inducting type of religious education have a decisive function. It opens up the subconscious levels of the children for the ultimate mystery of being.

But this advantage of the Church School would be lost if the primitive reception of the religious symbols were the end of the educational process at which one attempts to keep the pupils. This should never be tried. For very early the humanistic problem makes itself felt. As long as the pupil lives in a dreaming innocence of critical questions, he should not be awakened. But our time is not favorable for a long preservation of such innocence. And if the first critical questions are asked by the child, the first cautious answers must be given. Later on, the questions will become more critical, and the answers must become bolder and more fundamental.

The conquest of literalism without the loss of the symbols is the great task for religious education. It brings the humanistic element into the Church School and enables the pupil to remain in the unity of the Church as a mature, critical, and yet faith-determined personality. If the Church School is strong enough to take this humanistic principle into its own life, it can not only maintain its limited place in the present cultural situation, it can become increasingly important in our period of a growing tide of religious concern.

The problem of the Church School is more than the problem of a particular educational aim. It is the problem of the relation of Christianity and culture generally and Christianity and education especially. The problem is infinite and must be solved again in every generation. Within this frame, the Church School is like a small laboratory in which the large questions of Church and world can be studied and brought to a preliminary solution, a solution which could become an inestimable contribution to the solution of the larger problem.

III. CULTURAL COMPARISONS

XII

The Conquest of Intellectual
Provincialism: Europe and America

WHEN, soon after the victory of the Nazis in Germany and
after my removal from the chair of philosophy at the University of Frankfort, I decided to accept an invitation from
Union Theological Seminary in New York, I wrote to a friend
who had already left Germany: "There is everywhere in the
world sky, air, and ocean." This was my consolation in one
of the most tragic moments of my life. I did not write: "I can
continue everywhere my theological and philosophical work,"
because unconsciously I doubted whether one could do this
anywhere except in Germany. This is what I mean by the
term "provincialism" in the title of my paper. After having
lived for a few years in the United States and having worked
with theological and philosophical students and colleagues, I
became aware of this formerly unconscious provincialism;
and after having learned and taught several more years, the
provincial outlook began to recede. Today I hope that it has
disappeared, which does not mean that my German education
and the Continental European tradition which have shaped
me have become ineffective. If they had, this could mean that
I had fallen from one provincialism into another one, and that
I had become almost useless for the American intellectual
life, like some eager adoptionists amongst the refugees. But

this is the other point I want to make: America can save you from European and other provincialisms, but it does not necessarily make you provincial itself. There was and there still is a give and take in this country between traditions from all over the world, which makes the growth of an American provincialism extremely difficult. This is a summary of my experience and, I believe, of that of other theological and philosophical refugees. It underlies the following theoretical analyses which will deal first with the change of our scholarly outlook after over two decades of work in this country, and which will discuss secondly the elements in our tradition which America has been more and more ready to accept.

I.

If one studied theology in the first decade of this century at famous theological faculties within Germany, such as those of Tübingen, Halle, or Berlin, one identified the history of theology in the last four centuries with the history of German theology. It started with the Lutheran Reformation, it accepted or rejected elements of the thought of the Swiss Reformers, Zwingli and Calvin. It experienced the doctrinal legalism of classical orthodoxy, the enthusiastic subjectivism of the pietistic protest, the slow dissolution of the dogma of the Reformation and of the Christian dogma generally under the rational criticism of the philosophers of the Enlightenment and their theological pupils, the beginnings of historical criticism with respect to the Old and New Testaments—a movement in which the great Lessing, the classical representative of German Enlightenment, played the central role. Of course, one knew that there was an orthodox period in Western Calvinism as well as in German Lutheranism; but one considered its contribution not so much in the doctrinal as in the practical realms, in church and world politics, in personal and social ethics, things of which one always was and still is distrustful in German Lutheran theology. One also knew that there was pietism on Calvinist soil, that there was Methodism in England, and the Great Awakening in America. But one did not value very highly the theological contributions of evangelical enthusiasm and its pietistic successors. None of them was any competition for the classical tradition in theology. One also knew that the ideas of the Enlightenment originated in England and France and not in Germany. But one argued that in Catholic France they could be used only in the struggle against theology, not in support of it, and that British conformity was able to push the deistic criticisms of Bible and dogma into the background. It was our feeling that only in Germany was the problem of how to unite Christianity and the modern mind taken absolutely seriously.

All this was a mixture of limitation, arrogance, and some elements of truth. In the nineteenth century the belief that Protestant theology was German theology was not too far removed from the truth. The innumerable American theologians who studied in German universities in that century are witnesses to it. They usually speak more enthusiastically about the German theologians of their time than do the Germans themselves. It was the new foundation given to Protestant theology by Friedrich Schleiermacher that inaugurated this glorious period. It was the adaptation of Protestant theology to the modern mind by Ritschl and his widespread school that continued the leadership of German theology. When the greatest pupil of this school, Adolf Harnack, published his *Das Wesen des Christentums* (*What is Christianity?*) in the year 1900, it was translated into more languages than any other book except the Bible, and the Leipzig railway station was jammed by freight trains carrying Harnack's book all over the world. And when the reaction started against the theology of which Harnack's book is most representative, it was first Ernst Troeltsch in Germany and then Karl Barth in Switzerland and Germany who were the leaders. No wonder a German student of theology in the first decades of our century believed that Protestant theology is identical with German theology. It is not astonishing that he became provincial, since the province in which he lived was so large, important, and seemingly self-sustaining.

One may ask: Why did not philosophy change this attitude? The answer is simple: because German philosophy had the same attitude. Of course, it was impossible to overlook the fact that modern philosophy started in the Italy of the Renaissance, in the France of René Descartes, and the England of John Locke. One knew that the so-called philosophical century, namely the eighteenth, had its center in the France of Rousseau and Voltaire, and in the England of Berkeley and David Hume; one also realized that the great scientists of the seventeenth and eighteenth centuries were mostly French and English. But all this was overshadowed by Kant's philosophical criticism, by the rediscovery of Spinoza, by German classical philosophy as represented above all in Hegel's system, by the accompanying literature and poetry as represented above all in Goethe. It is symptomatic of the situation that we had the feeling—and here I speak autobiographically—that even Shakespeare, through the German translation by the Romanticist Wilhelm von Schlegel, had become German property. And this is not all. While, after the middle of the nineteenth century, school philosophy declined, a group of men arose who were to determine the destiny of the twentieth century: Schopenhauer, Nietzsche, and Marx, followed in the twentieth century by the fathers of

modern Existentialism, the translations of the Dane Kierkegaard, the cultural criticisms of the Swiss Burckhardt, the
anthropology of Jaspers, and the ontology of Heidegger. One
knew about Bergson in France and William James in America,
but one considered them as exceptions. And against them
stood the depth-psychological movement, the Viennese Freud,
the Swiss Jung, and the other schools, most of which grew on
German soil. Again the feeling arose that the philosophical
movement, at least after the year 1800, was centered in Germany, as once it was centered in Greece. Where the Greeks
came to an end, the Germans made a new beginning. The
German philosophers are the successors of the Greek philosophers. It was especially one trait in German philosophy
which, in our opinion, was the reason for its superiority: the
attempt to reunite, in a great synthesis, Christianity with the
modern mind. It was in its heart philosophy of religion, it was
Weltanschauung, a vision of the world as a whole. And we
despised every philosophy which was less than this.

Certainly we were aware that the literature, poetry, and
drama of the period, as distinct from that of the classical
period around the year 1800, had left Germany and had emi-
grated to the Russia of Gogol and Dostoyevsky, to the France
of Flaubert and Baudelaire, to the Sweden of Strindberg and
the Norway of Ibsen. But they all were available in German
translations and on German stages. They became parts of the
German cultural life and contributors to the German philosophical interpretation of the world.

And then it happened that at the end of the road of German
philosophy and theology, the figure of Hitler appeared. At
the time of our emigration it was not so much his tyranny and
brutality which shocked us, but the unimaginably low level
of his cultural expressions. We suddenly realized that if Hitler
can be produced by German culture, something must be

wrong with this culture. This prepared our emigration to this country and our openness to the new reality it represents. Neither my friends nor I myself dared for a long time to point to what was great in the Germany of our past. If Hitler is the outcome of what we believed to be the true philosophy and the only theology, both must be false. With this rather desperate conclusion we left Germany. Our eyes were opened, but they still were dull, unable to see the reality. So we came to this country.

II.

What did we see here? First, what did we see in theology? Many new things, indeed! Perhaps most important was the acquaintance with a quite different understanding of the relation between theory and practice. The independence of theory from any kind of practical application, as we were used to it in Germany, became questionable under the pragmatic-experiential approach of American theology. It was a partly disturbing, partly exciting experience when, after having read a most theoretical paper to an educated group, one was asked: What shall we do? This does not only mean: What is the practical consequence of the thing? It also means: What is the validity of the theory in the light of the pragmatic test? The background of this attitude generally, and in theology especially, is the emphasis on religious experience in the movements of evangelical radicalism which have largely formed the American mind and have made of experience a central concept in all spheres of man's intellectual life. The strong Calvinistic influence on the early periods of American history has contributed to the pragmatic approach by emphasizing the realization of the Kingdom of God in history over against the emphasis on pure doctrine in German Lutheranism. While in Continental Europe the theological faculties were the leaders of the Protestant churches, in American Protestantism the real power was in the hands of the presbytery or the corresponding bodies. Theology is not dismissed, but it is reduced to a secondary role in American Protestantism—a lesson we had to learn.

This structure of thought is not without influence on the content of theology. The glory of American theology lies neither in the historical nor in the dogmatic field, but in the sphere of social ethics. Everybody who knows something about the ecumenical movement and the structure of the World Council of Churches is aware of this fact. Whenever so-called Continental theology (meaning Continental European) clashes with Anglo-Saxon theology, it occurs in the realm of social ethics. The nature of Lutheran theology has prevented any strong development of this realm in German theological thought. Certainly the situation has changed with the rise of religious socialism and the theological support that Nazism received.

When, after the First World War, Germany was transformed by a political and social revolution of a rather radical character, the churches could not maintain their detached attitude toward politics. The King of Prussia who lost his throne was the *summus episcopus*—the supreme bishop of the Prussian Protestant church. This fall was a matter of existential concern for the church. The social groups who legally and spiritually had been the main supporters of Protestantism lost their power and were replaced by the professedly antireligious supporters of socialism. What should be the attitude of the church to the atheistic or completely indifferent masses whose representatives came into a power to which they never had been admitted before?

Religious socialism tried to give answers to those questions, but it could influence the traditionally conservative Lutheran churches only slightly. However, they could no longer dismiss the question of the relation between the Christian message and the social revolution. Even less could they avoid the problem put before them by the Nazi conquest of Germany and the attempt of the Nazi movement to draw the churches into the orbit of their neo-pagan ideas and practices. They had to fight against state interference and persecution by Nazi organizations inside and outside the church. They could not subject themselves to state authorities who actually were the representatives of a quasi-religious faith. But even this situation produced more a detachment of the churches from the political realm than the building of a positive social ethics. Finally, the recent split of mankind into two ideological and political camps, the democratic and the communist, has forced German theologians to discuss this situation in terms of principles. Even so, hesitation and uncertainty dominate Continental theology with respect to social ethics. Karl Barth, the leading theologian in European Protestantism, started as a religious socialist, turned since the period of his commentary on Paul's *Epistle to the Romans* in the early twenties against any kind of political theology, was forced into it again by Hitler's attack on the Protestant churches, and has returned to the attitude of detachment in the present East-West struggle. These oscillations are symptomatic of the difficulty in which Continental Protestantism finds itself with respect to a constructive social ethics.

As opposed to this character of Continental theology, American theological thinking is centered around social ethical problems. It surprised us to see how almost every theological problem was discussed in relation to the question of pacifism, how strong the religious color of the idea of democracy is, how the crusading spirit, in spite of all disappointments, never disappeared, how a whole period of theology was determined by the doctrines of the social gospel. The difficulties, stressed by Continental theology, in applying the absolute principles of the Christian message to concrete political situations, were met by American theological ethics in a rather ingenious way. One found that between the absolute principle of love and the ever-changing concrete situation, middle axioms exist which mediate the two. Such principles are democracy, the dignity of every man, equality before the law, etc. They are not unchangeable in the sense in which the ultimate principle is, but they mediate between it and the actual situation. This idea prevents the identification of the Christian message with a special political program. It makes it, on the other hand, possible for Christianity not to remain aloof from the actual problems of man's historical existence. In this way American theology has created a new approach to Christian social ethics, and has made the Christian message relevant not only to the relation of God and the individual person, but also to the relation of God and the world.

This attitude has presuppositions and consequences to discover, which is an ever new and exciting experience. The whole history of America has turned the American mind in a horizontal direction. The conquest of a vast country with a seemingly unlimited extension, the progressive actualization of the infinite possibilities in man's dealing with nature and himself, the dynamics of Calvinism and early capitalism, the freedom from a binding tradition and from the curses of European history—all this has produced a type of thinking which is quite different from the predominantly vertical thinking in Europe. The feudal system, which gives a predetermined place to everybody, admits only rare possibilities of horizontal progress. Life is a fight in the vertical line between divine and demonic forces. It is not a struggle for the progressive actualization of human possibilities. It is hardly necessary to say that such contrasts never are absolute, but they create a predominant attitude of great theological significance.

The European danger is a lack of horizontal actualization; the American danger is a lack of vertical depth. This is, for example, manifest in the way the Church is used and theology is understood. In Europe the problem of the Church is the problem of its ultimate foundation, and theology is supposed to explain this foundation in a completely balanced theological system. The Church is above all the institution for the salvation of souls, and theology the elaboration of ultimate truth about the way of salvation. Therefore preaching and the sacraments are decisive.

In American Christianity the Church is a social agent, among others, which tries to surpass the others in attractiveness. Its foundations are more or less taken for granted, but the practical demands, following from its nature, are in the center of interest. Making man better, helping him to become a person, and making the social conditions better, helping them to become actualizations of the Kingdom of God on earth—this is the function of the Church. Theology, in this view, has not so much the function of struggling for an adequate formulation of ultimate truth as of preparing theological students for their task as leaders of a congregation. This also must not be taken as an exclusive contrast. It is quite remarkable to see how in the last decades American theologians have tried to make theology scientifically respectable by applying experiential methods to it. It was an interesting attempt, although, I believe, not a very successful one. For what appeared in these theologies as the result of empirical research was actually the expression of conformity to non-Christian ideas.

This leads to another surprising discovery we made in American Protestantism: its world-wide horizons. The fact of the many denominational churches shows to everybody in an existential way that there are other possibilities of Protestant expression than one's own. It points back to different lines of church-historical development since the Reformation and before it. At the same time, Protestant provincialism is avoided by the fact that, for example, the Episcopal church has, in spite of its basically Protestant theology, preserved many Catholic elements in its way of life. One of the main problems of my theology—namely, Protestant principle and Catholic substance—arose out of this experience. It implies the question: How can the radicalism of prophetic criticism which is implied in the principles of genuine Protestantism be united with the classical tradition of dogma, sacred law, sacraments, hierarchy, cult, as preserved in the Catholic churches? I had to learn that when I used the word "Catholic" in a lecture, many listeners did not think, as every Continental listener would, of the Roman Catholic church. I had to realize that there are other churches which called themselves Catholic although they had accepted most of the doctrinal tenets of Protestantism. The question is a very serious one, in view of the inner difficulties of the Protestant churches, especially the danger in which they are of becoming a moral and educational institution beside others. But I can hardly imagine that the question in this form could have been conceived within Continental Protestantism.

The ecumenical point of view is further emphasized by the surprising fact that a Protestant institute such as Union Theological Seminary is intimately connected with a Greek Orthodox institute, St. Vladimir's Theological Seminary. At the same time, the opposite wing of Christian thought and life, Unitarianism, is in America a living reality and has still directly and even more indirectly a definite influence on the theological situation as a whole. The ecumenical point of view is also stressed by the fact that representatives of the so-called younger churches, those in Asia and Africa, are regular guests in the great American institutions of theological learning and ecclesiastical activity. They bring points of view into both American and Continental theology that were unknown to us within the limited horizon of German Protestantism.

Beyond all this it must be mentioned that the vivid exchange between America and the Far East, as well as the Near East, brings representatives of all great religions in a permanent stream to American universities and other institutions. This makes a Christian provincialism (not to be confused with the faith in the ultimacy of the Christian message) almost impossible. An existential contact with outstanding representatives of non-Christian religions forces one into the acknowledgment that God is not far from them, that there is a universal revelation.

In spite of the variety of points of view which permanently appear within the large horizon of American theology, this is not a struggle of everyone against everyone else, but discussion, competition, and teamwork. The actual unity of Protestantism, felt by most Protestant denominations, is symbolized in the many interdenominational theological seminaries and in the divinity schools of some great universities. It is alive in the co-operation of ministers of different denominations on the local level as well as in central organizations such as the National Council of Churches. It is expressed in a kind of Protestant conformity which is obvious to everybody who looks at it from outside the Protestant orbit. Theologically, this has led to a most radical interpenetration of denominational thinking, and beyond this it leads to the establishment of temporary or lasting organizations to which members of all the main denominations belong. This idea of theological team-work has deep roots in American life generally and the religious life especially. It stands in marked contrast to the isolated system-builders in Continental theology—again, a lesson not easy to learn.

The last point is as valid for philosophy as for theology. The philosophical approach to reality is experiential and, if possible, experimental. The validity of an idea is tested pragmatically, namely, by the function it has within the life process. This agrees with the question to which we have referred: What shall we do? The functional theory of truth is the abstract formulation of the often rather primitive way in which the question of the practical consequences of an idea is asked.

Behind the pragmatic approach to reality lies—mostly unknown to those who use it—one of the basic attitudes to reality which determined the medieval discussion, namely, nominalism. If one comes from the main tradition of Continental philosophy, one soon realizes how much these traditions are dependent upon what the Middle Ages called realism (which is nearer to modern idealism than to what today we call realism). In any case, it is not wrong to tell one's American students that they are nominalists "by birth."

A consequence of the nominalistic attitude is the feeling of standing at the periphery and not at the center of truth, and therefore the demand for tentative steps from the periphery towards the center, always aware of the fact that they are tentative and may lead in a wrong direction. This often produces an admirable attitude of humility, but sometimes complete rejection of a search for an ultimate truth. The positivistic, empirical attitude can be both a humble acknowledgment of man's finitude and an arrogant dismissal of the question of the truth which concerns us ultimately. This attitude makes understandable also the dominant role logical positivism has played in the last decades within the American philosophical scene. It can be interpreted as another expression of the humility of philosophers who want to avoid the idealistic claim that man is able to participate cognitively in the essential structure of reality.

But logical positivism can also be interpreted as the desire to escape problems which are relevant to human existence. It can be interpreted as the justified distrust of an interference of emotional elements with cognitive statements. But it also can be interpreted as the dismissal of existential problems into the non-cognitive sphere of feeling. The seriousness of this situation was one of the surprising discoveries we had to make when we came from traditions in which philosophy tries to build a system in which one can live. Certain words won an importance in America which they never had in Continental Europe: e.g. inquiry, investigation, research, project, etc. They all are symbolic of an attitude which is aware of one's not-having, and which has the courage to ask and to seek in order to have.

Courage is another important element in American philosophical thought. Perhaps one could say that the emphasis on becoming, process, growth, progress, etc., in American philosophy is the expression of a courage which takes upon itself risks, failures, regressions, disappointments in a way which one can hardly find in the groups which are mostly responsible for Continental philosophy. They rarely resist the temptation to escape into the vertical line when the horizontal line leads to a breakdown. It was and is a moving and transforming experience to observe examples of this American "courage to be"—individually and nationally. One asks: What is the spiritual substance out of which this courage and its philosophical and theological expressions are born?

III.

All this underlay what I have called theological and philosophical provincialism, Continental generally and German especially. The danger of the impression made upon us by these
attitudes and ideas was that they would push us into another
provincialism, an American one. But this is not the case. The
way in which we were received when we came as refugees to
the United States made it obvious that the intention on the
side of our American friends was not to Americanize us, but
to have us contribute in our own way to the over-all American
scene. Everyone was prepared for what we had to give, and
nobody demanded an assimilation in which our own experiences and ideas would be subdued.

I remember discussions among refugees in which an attitude
of quick assimilation was demanded by the one group while
the other group maintained an attitude of tenacious resistance
against adjustment to the new conditions. It was often not
easy to find a way between these extremes. And it would
have been impossible without the wisdom of some of our
American friends who, while helping us to adapt ourselves to
the new conditions, made it quite clear to us that they did
not want assimilation, but original creativity on the basis of
our traditions. This, it seems to me, was always so in America,
and it sometimes had the effect that older European traditions
were often more alive here than they were in Europe and
Germany. German Ritschlianism, for instance, was still a
strong force in American theology, when in Germany it had
lost most of its influence. Such things, and beyond them the
permanent influx of Asiatic ideas, make an American provincialism extremely unlikely.

Instead of being engulfed in American provincialism we
could bring to America ideas which have influenced and will

influence American thought in theology and philosophy. Without distinguishing the two, in the following survey I want to deal with some of the most conspicuous effects of the last immigration on the American intellectual life.

In the first place one must mention depth psychology—a concept which includes psychoanalysis but is much more embracing. The reasons for the astonishing victory of depth-psychological ideas in important groups of American society are manifold. One of them certainly is that they appeared in a psychotherapeutic context and not as abstract psychology, answering in this way the demand for pragmatic verification, which is so characteristic of the American mind.

Related to it and strongly supported by it was the recent reception of existentialist ideas. The threat of meaninglessness was increasingly felt, especially in the younger generation of students. Existentialism does not give the answer to the question of the meaning of existence, but formulates the question in all directions and in every dimension of man's being. The Existentialism of the twentieth century is not a special philosophy or the philosophy of a few European thinkers, but it is the mirror of the situation of the Western world in the first half of the twentieth century. It describes and analyzes the anxiety of our period as the special actualization of man's basic anxiety, the anxiety which is the awareness of his finitude.

Existentialism in alliance with depth psychology shows the psychological and sociological mechanisms which continually give occasion to the rise of such anxiety. It reveals the amount of doubt and cynicism about human existence which permeates the Western world. It is an expression of the courage to face meaninglessness as the answer to the question of meaning.

In spite of the strangeness of all this to the genuine American tradition of courage and self-affirmation, it could be received, especially in its artistic, poetic, fictional, and dramatic expressions. In this form its influence went beyond the educated groups, thus showing that the question of meaning is unconsciously present in many more people in the Western world than those who are able to articulate their anxiety and have the courage to take their anxiety upon themselves. It was and is possible for us who have experienced the rise of Existentialism in Europe to interpret its meaning to our American listeners in a genuine existential way.

American theology as a whole has strongly resisted the influx of neo-orthodoxy in its genuine form. But it has received many special ideas and emphases, especially if they appeared in a less supranaturalistic and authoritarian form than that developed by Barth, as for instance in Bultmann.

This refers, for instance, to the interpretation of history. Again, there are many causes for the decline of the progressivistic interpretation of history in American thought. There are the continual disappointments about the course of history from the end of the First World War up to the present events, day by day. But there is also the impact of the new understanding of human nature as it was introduced into America by the alliance of theological analysis, psychology, and Existentialist literature and art. In the fight against the utopia of progress the Europeans who had come to this country joined and strengthened the anti-utopian forces which were latently present in genuine American groups and personalities —as for example, Reinhold Niebuhr.

Historical consciousness generally was something we brought from historically minded Europe to unhistorically minded America. It is not a matter of historical knowledge, but a matter of a feeling which every European instinctively has, namely, that ideas are in their very nature historical. The development of an idea is an essential element in the idea itself.

This is the background of what was called *Geistesgeschichte* (inadequately translated "intellectual history" or "history of thought"). The true meaning of *Geistesgeschichte* is not a factual history of former thoughts, but is the attempt to make visible the implications and consequences of an idea in the light of its history. In this sense *Geistesgeschichte* is a part of systematic philosophy and theology. The assertion is rather unfamiliar to most American students, and it was one of our most important tasks to balance the American emphasis on new beginning with the European emphasis on tradition. And it was equally important to balance the American emphasis on facts with the European emphasis on interpretation.

The question we ask ourselves after over two decades of participation in the American spiritual life is: Will America remain what it has been to us, a country in which people from every country can overcome their spiritual provincialism? One can be both a world power politically and a provincial people spiritually. Will the emphasis on the "American way of life" produce such a situation? There is a serious danger that it will. The America to which we came was wide open. It liberated us without restricting us to new spiritual limitations. For this America we shall fight against any groups working for American provincialism, and we shall work for an America in which every provincialism, including theological and philosophical provincialism, is resisted and conquered.

XIII
Religion in Two Societies:
America and Russia

AN ANALYSIS of the function of religion in a society must include both public religion (religion in the narrow sense) and religion of the heart (religion in the larger sense) in an inseparable interdependence. Some important insights follow from this consideration. First, the larger concept of religion is not identical with the retreat to subjective religiousness, to emotion without content, and to morality without devotion. The larger concept, like the narrower one, includes both organized religion and religion of the heart.

As discussed earlier in this book, religion in the larger sense of the word, is the state of being ultimately concerned. Such an ultimate concern is real in the individual; it is also embodied in the institutions of a society and effective in the actions of social groups. Divine beings may be symbols of an ultimate concern, but they are not the only possible symbols. The early Christians were accused of atheism because they eliminated the pantheon of pagan gods for the sake of the ground of all being. Their God was not *a* being, but the power of being which gives Being to every being. This idea of God was too radical for pagan theism, and it is too radical for some kinds of Christian theism which are preached and taught every day in many Christian churches. It is, however, true to the idea of God as a symbol of what concerns us ultimately.

For two centuries men have experienced the disintegration of the symbols of ultimate concern in their particular religious tradition, or they have experienced the change of their own ultimate concern without being able to express the new experience in adequate symbols. But there is no vacuum in spiritual life, as there is no vacuum in nature. An ultimate concern must express itself socially. It cannot leave out any sphere of human existence. Intended or not, it expresses itself in the most basic of all cultural creations, in human language, and thence it permeates the whole life of a society.

The language of those for whom their religious traditions had become obsolete was secular. The alternative was not another religion, as in the period of Diocletian, but secular science, the secular state, secular art, secular ways of life, as they arose in the Renaissance. If one applies the narrower concept of religion, secular language is opposed to religious language. If one applies the larger concept of religion, secular language hides as well as expresses a religious concern. And we must use such language if we speak in the middle of the twentieth century about religion in two societies.

CHURCH AND STATE IN RUSSIA AND AMERICA

Before examining this more complex phase of the subject, let us compare the present status of the Church in a totalitarian and in a democratic society, in Russia and in the United States. The lack of adequate information concerning the situation of the Eastern Church makes it difficult to give more than a few hints. According to information received by the World Council of Churches, for example, the religious life in the Russian Orthodox Church is by no means at an end, but it is greatly restricted in range and influence. Education, public discussion, and propaganda of every kind by the Church are prohibited. The number of church buildings has been drastically reduced. But there is no persecution, as there was in some phases of Soviet history. Today the political authorities are not interested in the propaganda of that religious atheism which attacked the Eastern Orthodox Church in Russia with the fanaticism with which hostile churches used to fight each other. On the contrary, the Soviet authorities are interested in using the Church as a way of satisfying psychological needs which otherwise could become dangerous to the political structure. The Orthodox clergy has been criticized for accepting this role. And there is no doubt that in a situation like that in which the Eastern Church finds itself today, human weakness makes its appearance as it did in the periods of persecution in the early Church. But this is not the whole truth.

There is a tradition in Eastern Christianity which is called Cesaro-Papism, the identification of the highest ecclesiastical authority with the authority of the emperor or the king. The ruler is considered as the Christ of his nation, e.g. Constantine was buried with the symbolic tombs of the twelve apostles around him. The Czar was the protector of the Holy Synod and therefore the ruler of the Church. And in order to show that the two societies which we are contrasting in this chapter have certain points in common, we should mention that the churches of the Lutheran Reformation established the prince of the territory as *summus episcopus*, the supreme bishop of his territory. Also, in England, as far back as the twelfth century, the so-called Anonymous of York fought for the identification of the King of England with the Christ of his nation, opposing the papal authority over the English clergy.

All this is important for an understanding of the present predicament of the Russian Orthodox Church. It is nothing new in its tradition that the earthly ruler rules the Church also. But this fact has not the significance that it has in the West. The Eastern Church is a Church of sacramental mysticism. It is not a Church with social and political ideals. The points of a possible conflict are limited. No Czar could easily have changed one letter of the liturgical tradition, but if a bishop had used the Christian doctrine for criticizing the social and political structure of the State, the Czar would have annihilated him instantly. It does not seem that the attitude of the Soviet authorities is much different, except that the Russian leaders would not accept the honor of becoming the protector of the Holy Synod.

We in this country accept the separation of Church and State, the final outcome of the struggle of the evangelistic Dissenters of the Reformation against both the Roman and the Protestant churches. We are proud of this heritage, and religious freedom is included in all enumerations of the freedoms we enjoy. Lately some questions have arisen about the meaning of this separation. Many people have the feeling that things went too far. The sphere in which this doubt has appeared is education. It is felt that secular education in most of our schools is not neutral education, but is biased by an "anti-religious religion." If, however, the State should support a "religious religion" in education, even in a very limited way, would this not be the end of the separation of Church and State? It is not astonishing that the problem is similar in both societies under consideration, because this is a problem of every society. Who shall educate? Or, more precisely, who educates the educators?

The problem was not very urgent so long as that remarkable Anglo-Saxon feature, conformity, was dominant in American religious life. It was the non-conformists of the old continent who, when they came to this country, established, first by violent measures, then by tolerance, a new conformity. This conformity is still real, as a newcomer can probably see more clearly than a native American. Furthermore, it endeavors to become universal despite almost insuperable difficulties, and it is the driving force in ecumenical co-operation, not only of American denominations, but of all creeds including Eastern Orthodoxy.

But organized Protestantism means something more than this in the democratic society of the United States. In contrast to the mystical, sacramental self-restriction of Eastern Orthodoxy, it is a social power of the highest degree. Through the democratic processes it influences political decisions, social ideals, ways of life, international actions. And this is equally true of the Roman Church, which, as the largest single Church in this country and as a tightly-organized authoritarian group, is more powerful than any particular Protestant denomination and, in some respects, than all Protestants together. It is the principle of tolerance which makes this power possible, and it is one of the paradoxes of Protestantism in this country that it must be tolerant towards those who by their very nature must destroy tolerance at the moment when the tolerant processes of democracy have brought them into power.

MARXISM, RELIGION, AND EASTERN SOCIETY

We must now turn to an analysis of the hidden religious powers in East and West. How was it possible that Marxism should have overcome most of the eastern part of the Christian world, and how did it happen that Marxism was transformed into Stalinism a few decades after its victory? There are many answers to these questions and none of them excludes the others. It is our task to try to penetrate these mysterious and most important phenomena from the point of view of religion in the larger sense, the state of being ultimately concerned.

Eastern Christianity early became a religion of mysticism and sacraments. It represents the one type of religion which we find everywhere in history, the type which emphasizes the presence of the Holy, the sacramental and mystical union with the Divine, the intuition of the Divine as it is here and there manifest as the spiritual depth of all things in nature and history. It is a religion of visual beauty, of liturgical perfection, of theological speculation, of mystical elevation. It is not a religion of social and political action and transformation. It transcends the given state of things without trying to change it.

But the Holy is not only that which is; the Holy is also that which ought to be, that which demands justice above all. If, therefore, a religion neglects its social and political implications, a reaction of the neglected side occurs and may be not only victorious over but also destructive of the whole sacramental system. This happened when the Islamic invasion overwhelmed vast sections of the Byzantine Empire, especially those where sacramentalism had deteriorated into magic superstition, as for instance, in Egypt. In comparison with this type of deteriorated Christianity, Islamic puritanism and legalism were superior. Its main interest was the organization and education of societies, often on the lowest level of culture.

Some of the Byzantine emperors tried to save their empire from the onslaught of Islam by purifying the Christian cult of the superstitious use of pictures of Christ and the saints, the so-called icons. These attempts neither saved the empire from Islamic radicalism and fanaticism, nor did they prevail in the Church against the traditionalists. Russian Christianity was not influenced by them. It became a non-social, sacramental, and mystical type of religion, and after centuries it suffered the same fate as the other Eastern churches. It was conquered by another social movement of puritan character and fanatical faith, namely Marxism.

Marxism, in the frame of this chapter means neither Stalinism nor Leninism nor Marxism after Marx; it does mean the genuine impulses in the thinking and acting of Marx himself. If understood in this sense, Marxism is a movement of social justice against a conservative system of political and ecclesiastical hierarchies which were identical at the top and worked together on every level. Like the iconoclastic emperors of Byzantium the Czar tried to avert the threatening attack, partly by a suppression of potential foes, partly by social reforms. But it was too late. The system broke down under the impact of communist radicalism. It was a conquest from within, not by an irreligious system but by a religion of social justice in secular terms. It was the type of ultimate concern for which justice is the measure of truth, as it was for the prophets, for Jesus, for Mohammed, for some radical sects of the Reformation on the Continent and in England, for the bourgeois revolutionaries of the eighteenth century, for the founders of the United States, for the pre-Marxian socialists, and for Marx himself.

Without this background the meaning of the Russian Revolution cannot be understood. However decisive may have been the actual circumstances—the unimaginable amount of social injustice, the breakdown after the First World War, the economic and technical backwardness—one thing is not explained by all this. That is, the infinite concern of those who under tremendous suffering had prepared the revolution and carried it through. In terms of the larger concept of religion, one must say that it was an ultimate concern about the transformation of reality which overcame an ultimate concern about the consecration of reality. Or, in more technological terms, it was, in a secular and atheistic cloak, the eschatological striving for the coming kingdom of God which conquered the sacramental union with the always-present God.

But the one side is not possible without the other. It is impossible to live on the "ought to be" alone. Every revolution devours not only its own children but itself as well. In order to preserve its results, the revolution must become conservative. Sacramental or quasi-sacramental ideas, rites, institutions must be established, actualized, and defended. New hierarchies develop; traditions, especially national ones, are revived. Persons, words, and institutions are consecrated. They become symbols of the ultimate concern which permeates the whole society. But it is not simply a restoration of the past that occurs in this stage of the development. Many elements of the revolutionary period are preserved. The messianic impetus survives and is turned towards the rest of the world. It creates a permanent threat to other nations and calls forth their reactions to this threat. The ideas of social justice with which the attack on the sacramental system was won are repeated, although the original situation no longer exists. They have become slogans and tools of propaganda, inside and outside the system. The secular attitude and language is unchanged, but it is combined in a peculiar way with a strong national mysticism.

Today one rejects the cosmopolitan implications of Marxist rationalism. A similarity with the ideas of the Slavophiles of the nineteenth century is manifest. As they believed that the disintegrating West must be saved by the spiritual substance which is preserved in Eastern Christianity, so the present Russian Byzantinism combines an unlimited contempt for the autonomous cultures of the West with a belief in its own saving power. But in contrast to the Slavophiles, this feeling is cloaked in a terminology which is taken from the autonomous philosophical movements of the West.

And even more, this Russian Byzantinism uses the most refined methods of the technical control of nature and society in order to maintain and increase its power. It uses terror in a way which never would have been possible without the triumph of technical reason in Western culture. At the same time it moves masses of people outside Russia with its revolutionary eschatology, and it holds the Russian masses partly by terror, partly by a mystical Neo-Byzantinism of Russian provenience. It seems that without a religious analysis of the Russian situation it is impossible to understand the paradoxes of totalitarian Russia. Furthermore, it is sometimes justifiable to forget propaganda and to look into the deeper levels of such a historical reality as the Communist society.

MARXISM, RELIGION, AND WESTERN SOCIETY

The same method must be applied to an analysis of our own society. As in the case of Russia, we must, for the sake of this inquiry, forget for a moment the propaganda against that country, so in the case of America, must we forget the propaganda for America. This does not change the fact that this analysis itself is a product of Western autonomous thought, scientific method, and liberal tolerance. But to be aware of this fact does not mean to abstain from a critical analysis of our own existence in the light of the larger concept of religion.

We have referred to the conformity of the Anglo-Saxon society. It consists in present-day America of a combination of the spirit of Protestantism and of scientific humanism. The

Catholic Church, in spite of its political power, has not deeply influenced the character of this conformity. An analysis of American conformity shows that it is rooted in common traits of early as well as of late Western Christianity; namely, the emphasis on personality and history, and correspondingly the religious interest in social ethics and politics. We have seen that out of this tradition came developments which in their Marxist form finally conquered the Eastern part of Christianity. Although originating in the West, Marxism could not conquer the West. This is due to the fact that the sectarian movements of the Middle Ages and the Reformation, as well as the bourgeois revolution of the eighteenth and nineteenth centuries, have realized many elements of the program which came to the East as a new and saving message.

The question of Western society, seen in the light of religion as the state of ultimate concern, is not communism but the disintegration of its democratic conformity and a possible authoritarian reaction to it. This can be shown in relation to the Protestant as well as to the humanist element in it. The religious autonomy which is implied in the Protestant principle, and the cultural autonomy which is implied in the humanist principle, are continually threatened by the self-estrangement of human nature. This is the great theme of the Existentialists. They ask a question and insist that this question is asked profoundly. It is the old religious question of the human predicament, man's finitude and self-estrangement, his anxiety and despair. They revolt against the increasing transformation of man into a thing, a cog in the universal system of organized production and organized consumption. They react against the education of adjustment which tries to press everyone into a pattern by exposing him day and night to centrally directed means of communication. Although in anti-religious, atheistic, often cynical, often despairing terms, they represent an ultimate religious concern; they see the truth about the human predicament universally and in every particular situation.

This question in its radical form can no longer be silenced in the Western world. On the answer to it depends the spiritual and largely the political destiny of the West. Will there be a way to avoid a totalitarian reaction against the disintegration of which the Existentialist question is both a symptom and a possible remedy? To suppress this question is not a way out; to join the Eastern solution, even less. But the very nature of the Holy points the way out. It has two sides: the holiness of what ought to be, the sacramental and the personal, the mystical; and the social side, the mystery and the reasonableness of being. Will we be able to find a new union of these elements in a creative synthesis in which we take the spiritual substance of the East into the personal and social forms of the West? This is our question.

XIV

An Evaluation of Martin Buber:
Protestant and Jewish Thought

THE purpose of this chapter is not to evaluate the work of Buber—this has been done and will be done by others more competent for the task—but to show what Protestant theology has received and should receive from his religious message and theological ideas. My conviction is that it is much. Of course, this conviction is dependent on my own theological point of view and on the amount of influence Buber has had directly and, even more, indirectly on my thought. Therefore I cannot speak for Protestant theology as such, but only for my understanding of it.

But I know that in all the points I make here there are many Christian theologians and laymen who will agree with me and with my valuation of Buber's significance for Protestantism.

I see this significance in three main directions: Buber's existential interpretation of prophetic religion, his rediscovery of mysticism as an element within prophetic religion, and his understanding of the relation between prophetic religion and culture, especially in the social and political realms. Here, too, in each case it is not a report about Buber's position as a whole or about its development that I wish to give, but a description of the Protestant theological situation in so far as it has shown itself receptive to his central ideas.

I.

My first point is the latest in Buber's development. It is explained systematically in his book *I and Thou*, a most important and influential philosophy of religion—if this term can be used for a small book which is at least as much a religious pronouncement as it is a cognitive analysis. Buber's interpretation of religion can be called "existential."

An interpretation of religion is existential if it emphasizes the two-way character of every genuine religious experience: the involvement of the whole man in the religious situation, and the impossibility of having God outside this situation. The function of the phrase "and Thou" is to express this character of the religious experience in a radical and concrete way.

Buber distinguishes the "I-Thou" relationship from the "I-It" relationship. This distinction contains the main problem of Existentialism, namely, how to be or to become an "I" and not an "It," how to be or to become a person and not a thing, how to be or to become free and not determined. Long before the recent existential thinking appeared, Buber had asked and answered these questions on the basis and by the power of prophetic religion: there is no other way of becoming an "I" than by meeting a "Thou" and by accepting it as such, and there is no other way of meeting and accepting a "Thou" than by meeting and accepting the "eternal Thou" in the finite "Thou."

But this relation stands under the tragic fate of being continuously transformed into an "I-It" relation. The "Thou" becomes a thing, and is put by us into time and space and under the law of causality. The relation in which both sides are completely involved has become a detached relation; God no less than man, and man no less than tree, become things, objects, and the "I" becomes a subject looking at them, but not in a full relation with them. Only a part of one's being, the cognitive or the practical interest, is involved. It is our "melancholic fate" that this happens eternally, that it has happened since the beginning of human history and that it will last as long as man has conscious life.

Protestant theologians have been deeply impressed by these ideas of a religious Existentialism—which are perhaps less original and less powerful than those of Kierkegaard, but which are also less paradoxical and less forced. But the weight of both the orthodox and the liberal tradition in Protestantism was too great to admit Buber's ideas to the full influence they deserve.

Liberal Protestant theology, since the rise of Deism, has tried to mediate between the world interpreted by modern science and the biblical idea of God. This, of course, is the task of theology, and Kierkegaard and Buber are no less mediating theologians than Ritschl and Rauschenbusch. But the question is: how to mediate? And if this question is asked the answer must be: liberal Protestantism has adapted the God of the Bible to the It-world of modern technical civilization. This It-world, this realm of unrelated objectivity, of mere things, embraces nature as well as man, and man individually as well as socially. Nature is, in the classical Newtonian view, a whole of totally determined bodies, moving according to quantitatively measureable laws. An "I-Thou" relation to a natural object is impossible in such a view of nature, because man controls nature for his own purposes. God becomes a "limiting concept," which means that he is removed to the utter limits of nature, unable to interfere with it. The same principles were progressively applied to man and society by scientific psychology and sociology. The individual person became subjected to the great machine of production and consumption, and he himself became a machine subjected to the law of stimulus and response. The "I-Thou" relation is delivered over to emotion and subjective feeling.

Liberal Protestantism saw the danger of this situation for religion and culture, but it was unable to cope with it. Protestant apologetics tried to show that within the whole of things there is a place for a divine being, and that personality and active interrelation with the world must be attributed to it. "Empirical theology" tried to show that this being can be approached with the general methods of scientific research. Historical inquiries were supposed to give the foundation of faith; religion was to elevate the moral personality over the nature in us and around us. The meaning of history was seen in the progressive establishment of a society in which peace and justice governed. All these ideas, however, remain, in Buber's terms, within the realm of the "I-It" relation. They try to transcend the It-world, but they do not succeed because they have accepted it at the beginning. They do not break through the ultimate presuppositions of the It-determined modern world view, and therefore they have no power to interpret convincingly the divine-human relationship. Buber's existential "I-Thou" philosophy reaches the very depths of the situation and should be a powerful help in reversing the victory of the "It" over the "Thou" *and* the "I" in present civilization.

Such a help cannot come from old or new orthodoxy. It is easy to use Kierkegaard's and the other Existentialists' protests against the It-determined attitude of our time for the sake of religious and cultural reaction. Buber also can and has been used in this way. But he permanently tries to show that orthodoxy (or liturgical traditionalism) does ultimately what liberal theology does: it transforms the "I-Thou" relation into an "I-It" relation. Wherever the "eternal Thou" can be manipulated, whether by rational or by irrational methods, whether by morals or by dogmas or by cults, the divine "Thou" has become an "It" and has lost its divinity.

The "I-Thou" philosophy of Martin Buber, challenging both orthodox and liberal theology, points to a way beyond their alternatives.

II.

Buber was deeply influenced by mystical traditions outside and inside Judaism, and he himself has in many ways contributed to the interpretation of mystical ideas and movements. His discovery of the significance of genuine Hasidism was decisive for his development and greatly influenced the general religious and theological atmosphere in the first quarter of this century.

While Catholicism, by its very nature, is able to include the mystical tradition within itself and has done so from early times to the present, Protestantism, like Judaism, has a naturally ambiguous relation to mysticism. Both belong to the prophetic personalistic type of religion, and both had to fight during the whole history against magic, sacramentalism, and depersonalizing ecstasy. On the other hand, there is no living religion in which the principle of mysticism, the immediate presence of the divine and the way of union with it, is not thought and practiced. Ecstatic and visionary experiences are abundant in the prophetic literature and in orthodox Jewish teaching. Orthodox Protestantism knew the doctrine of "mystical union" (*unio mystica*) and produced, from its very beginning, pietistic movements within itself. Whether it was the doctrinal, the ethical, or the mystical element that came into the foreground was not a matter of religious principle but of personal and historical conditions.

But this is not the whole story. Both Judaism and Protestantism have developed within themselves forms of mysticism which were considered by representatives of their respective orthodox, as well as liberal, theologies as trespassing the limits of what is possible on the basis of prophetism. Nineteenth-century Protestantism developed an especially strong anti-mystical feeling in connection with its capitulation before the I-determined modern world view. In the Kant-Ritschlian school of Protestant theology, which dominated the second half of the 19th century in Europe as well as in this country, mysticism was considered the arch-enemy of genuine Protestantism. Pietism was considered as a Catholic remnant, the "mystical union" was criticized as un-Protestant, a purge even of those mystical elements which are implicit in metaphysics was attempted. The Christian message was measured by moral standards and adapted to the demands of a rational and sober control of nature and a corresponding organization of society.

It was this anti-mystical bias which, in contrast to many other elements of liberal theology, has been taken over by the so-called neo-Orthodox leaders of present-day Protestant theology. But mysticism also found defenders in 20th-century Protestantism: the rediscovery of the idea of the Holy by Rudolph Otto, the influence of Eastern Orthodox Christianity mediated by Dostoyevsky and the Russian refugees after the First World War, the intensive interest in the great mystics of East and West, the liturgical movements, the new understanding of sacraments and symbols, the new rise of metaphysical thinking and of corresponding artistic expressions—all these made it necessary for Protestant theology to take the question of mysticism much more seriously and to deal with it much more affirmatively than it did in the previous one hundred years.

In this situation Buber's reinterpretation of Hasidism is extremely valuable. It shows the possibility of a mysticism which does not contradict but which intensifies prophetic religion. Original Hasidism grew up in Polish Judaism in the middle of the 18th century. It was a movement which kept strictly within the frame of Jewish tradition. It did not want to reform but to intensify. Jewish mysticism as embodied in the Kabbala was effectively included in it, but in such a way that the neo-Platonic elements of the Kabbala, the valuation of ecstasy and religious metaphysics, were strongly reduced in significance. They did not disappear: ecstatic experiences, complete union with God, were not denied. But since they were restricted to rare moments, it was daily life and work in which the divine was encountered. Man, it was asserted, must become a unity in the encounter with the divine unity. But he cannot merge into the divine One. The "I-Thou" relation between man and the "eternal Thou" cannot be transcended, at least not in this life. Therefore the mystical union is man's union with himself and with God for action, for the life in this world, and for the recognition of the divine ground in everything.

Religion, for Hasidism as well as for Buber, is consecration of the world. It is neither acceptance of the world as it is, nor bypassing the world in the direction of a transcendent divine, but it is consecration in the double sense of seeing the divine in everything.

This attitude removes the dualism of a holy and a secular sphere. In spite of the observance of doctrine and cult, in spite of its emphasis on the continuous conversation between the individual soul and God in prayer and meditation, the decisive characteristic of Hasidic religion is its way of looking at the world and acting in it. For man's action in the world has significance not only for man but also for God. Man is responsible for the destiny of God in so far as God is in the world; man is called to re-establish the broken unity in himself and in the world. God waits for man, and the answer to man's action is divine grace. Man's action is not by way of asceticism or extraordinary deeds. It is the consecration of the moment, it is the simple act which is demanded from a special individual in a special situation, it is the acting of the anonymous people, the children and the simple ones. Such acting, if it is done in consecration, prepares the coming of the Kingdom of God. It is messianic action.

Buber, who in his first encounter with Hasidism was attracted by its purely mystical side, came to realize more and more the significance of the active side. And while in the introduction to his collection of mystical sayings, *Ekstatische Konfessionen*, he emphasized the union with God in which the differences of God, world, and self disappear, he later sharply criticized the "doctrine of absorption." It is, according to him, not lived reality and is therefore the most refined expression of the "It." The doctrine of absorption is the attempt to get rid of the "Thou" and consequently of the "I." It annihilates the world and loses the "eternal Thou." It is a possibility on the brink of being—Buber has not denied this—but he has denied its ultimate significance. Significant is the daily life and the union the "I" achieves in the encounter with the "eternal Thou," and the radiation into the world of him who is united in himself.

A serious consideration of this way of solving the problem of "mysticism and prophetic religion" by Protestant theology would help it avoid many futile discussions and the elaboration of untrue contrasts. It is not true that mysticism and prophetic religion contradict each other. The thought and the reality of Buber are witness to this.

III.

If Buber's mysticism had separated him from his prophetic tradition, he could not have joined the religious socialist movement. Of course, he never was a politically active member of the small group of men and women who called themselves religious socialists in postwar Germany, but he was a friend and adviser of the movement. His ideas about the relation of the religious encounters between the "I" and the "eternal Thou" to the cultural encounters between the "I" and the human "Thou" are worth the attention of Protestant theologians.

One of the most difficult problems for Protestant theology is that of social ethics (including politics, foreign relations, economics, education). Roman Catholicism has an authoritative system of social ethics. Orthodox Judaism has developed one out of the Torah. Protestantism has neither a Torah in the Jewish sense, nor a classical system of ethics in the Catholic sense. It is, especially in its Lutheran form, more spiritualistic than both of them. It pronounces the ethics of love and believes that the inner side of all human relations can be ordered by the spirit of love, while the external side must be ordered by the repressive power of the state. The work of the state, it says, is not opposed to love because its sword serves ultimately the Kingdom of God by keeping down the evildoers, but it is a "strange," "improper" work of love that is performed in this way. It is therefore impossible to derive from the religious sphere rules to which the state must subject itself, and requests that the church could make upon the state. This makes the state independent of the ultimate human relation— to God. The state must be obeyed even if its rulers and institutions are bad. Revolution must be denied under all circumstances.

It is understandable that such an attitude completely estranged a revolutionary group like German labor from churches and religion and produced a gap between the masses of the workers and the religious tradition, even in its liberalized form. Many people were deeply concerned about this situation, and when, after the First World War, labor participated in the control of the state, religious socialism tried to close that fateful gap. But before it could succeed, the forces of reaction and fascism took over and destroyed the movement, expelling, killing, or suppressing its representatives.

The question facing the religious socialists was: on what theological basis can religion support socialism or any other concrete political and social idea? It was, of course, impossible for someone who had acquired even the slightest insights into the origin of Christianity to make Jesus into a socialist or to confuse the prophetic message with an economic program. And it is equally impossible to derive concrete laws of political behavior from any biblical statements. The Bible, especially the New Testament, does not give institutional commandments or advice. And if it does so (or seems to do so) it is dependent on the historical situation in which it was written. Religious socialism, therefore, emphasized that socialism is the demand of the concrete situation of late industrial society, if seen in the light of the principles of love and justice. This, however, is a matter of judgment by individual Christians and cannot become a doctrine of the church. The church has to pronounce the principles and to criticize the given reality in the light of these principles, but it cannot decide about their concrete application. At least the Protestant church cannot. It must leave this to the courage, intuition, and risk of voluntary groups.

It is obvious that from the point of view of Buber, especially of his "I-Thou" philosophy, this is the only permissible attitude toward concrete cultural and social questions. Buber, like all religious socialists, accepts the criticism of bourgeois society by Marx while rejecting the anti-religious bias of Marxism. He accepts, with all religious socialists, Marx's doctrine of the self-estrangement of man in modern capitalism, his becoming a "thing," a quantitatively calculable piece of working power; but, like all religious socialists, he rejects the belief of Marxism that a special group, the proletariat, its revolutionary victory, and the new institutions following this victory, will bring about a change in human nature. This, obviously, would be thinking in terms of the "I-It" pattern and would mean the loss of the "Thou." Buber, from his presuppositions, had to start with the single "I-Thou" relation and enlarge it to what is called in German *Gemeinschaft* (community), the living unity of a group which has a common spiritual basis and a genuine "I-Thou" relation between its members. Socialism is real in such communities. It cannot be produced by the state, but only by small groups who realize socialism in themselves and go towards it in their personal life and in the power of their common center, the relation to the "eternal Thou." *Gemeinschaft* is a messianic category, and socialism acts in the direction of the messianic fulfillment; it is a messianic activity to which everybody is called.

This, of course, is a highly spiritualistic interpretation of religious socialism which agrees to a great extent with the spiritualistic attitude towards social ethics in early Protestantism. The question for Protestant theology, therefore, cannot be whether it is wrong—it certainly is not—but whether it is sufficient. And again I would say, it certainly is not. It leaves the state, the political power, almost completely to the "demons," to an absolutized "I-It" relationship. Such a surrender is not warranted. Even the state has potentialities for an "I-Thou" relationship. It can be considered as one of those spiritual forms which for Buber belong to the third type of "I-Thou" relation. And there is no reason why this should not be so, if everything created is included in the divine and can be consecrated. Here is the point over which the religious socialists disagreed with Buber, and it is the reason why he kept himself at the fringe of the movement.

It is for the same reason that Buber in his relation to the Zionist movement was always in a special position. He affirmed it as a messianic attempt to create *Gemeinschaft*, while he negated it as a political attempt to create a state. History, however, seems to show that without the shell of a state, a community cannot exist.

There are many other points in which Buber's significance for Protestant theology is manifest—for instance, his doctrines of the "word," of myth and symbol, of the meaning of art. But the three points developed in this article seem to me the most important and most embracing. They show that the interrelation and conversation, the "I-Thou" encounter of Judaism and Christianity, has not yet, and never should, come to an end.

IV. CONCLUSION

XV

Communicating the Christian Message: A Question to Christian Ministers and Teachers

THE question implied in this chapter is not: What is the Christian message? Rather it is: How shall the message (which is presupposed) be focused for the people of our time? In other words, we are concerned here with the question: *How can the Gospel be communicated?* We are asking: How do we make the message heard and seen, and then either rejected or accepted? The question *cannot* be: How do we communicate the Gospel so that others will accept it? For this there is no method. To communicate the Gospel means putting it before the people so that they are able to decide for or against it. The Christian Gospel is a matter of decision. It is to be accepted or rejected. All that we who communicate this Gospel can do is to make possible a genuine decision. Such a decision is one based on understanding and on partial participation.

We all know the pain we suffer when we meet people who reject the Gospel, although they have no authority for rejecting it, or meet other people who were not able to make a genuine decision about it, since the Gospel was never properly communicated to them. Another experience which is but slightly less painful is to meet those who have accepted it without ever having been able to make a decision about it because it never was a matter of doubt. It came to them as a matter of habit, custom, or social contact. This the Gospel can never be.

True communication of the Gospel means making possible a definite decision for or against it. We who communicate the Gospel must understand the others, we must somehow participate in (their) existence so that their rejection means partly an ejection, a throwing it out in the moment in which it starts to take root in them. To this point we can bring them, and this is what communicating the Gospel means.

I.

We then come to the question: Where are the people living to whom we are to communicate the Gospel in such a way that they are able to make a genuine decision?

There is one general answer, one we can give immediately. *They all participate in human existence.* This is a very universal answer. But it is by no means a simple answer. Let us think about some of the implications of participating in human existence.

For example, we speak about the *anxiety* of being finite, of being subject to fate and destiny, of having to die. Ministers deal with this in sermons. But suppose we state this as a general implication of all human existence, and someone speaks for the people in India and says, "Such a statement about anxiety does not fit in India where the kind of anxiety about death which we find in the Western world does not prevail." Or suppose we speak of our feelings of *guilt* as an implication of all human existence. A protest is likely to come from our modern psychologists who say, "Every feeling of guilt is due to neurosis produced in our early years or to some other individual or social cause, and it can be removed. It is not characteristic of human nature." Or, in the third place, suppose we speak, in view of the world situation, of man's tragic existence. In the moment we say that this is characteristic of the human situation, somebody will assert that this situation is based on special unfavorable circumstances which in the process of history will be removed. The critics may unite against us and say that what we imply about human existence is not universal, but is contingent upon the space and period in which man lives. These critics insist that a universal answer cannot be given in view of the varied environments of people, and that we may not speak of human nature and destiny as if these were universal. There is only one thing which is universal, they would say, and that is the fact that man is changeable, that he is open to infinite historical transformations, that man can and must make himself. If we take these arguments seriously, what kind of gospel can we communicate? If it is true that the biblical and ecclesiastical Gospel presupposes a special type of man, a special nature and existence of man, what is our gospel?

As Christian theologians we do not believe that these people are right. We believe that even if we reduce the universal nature of man to changeability in history, enough can yet be said about man to justify our interpretation of human nature. Now this *is* theoretically possible, and we have done it. But what shall we tell those people who feel that they have not the nature of that kind of man to whom the Gospel speaks? That is something which happens to us all the time.

The first thing we must do is to communicate the Gospel as a message of man understanding his own predicament. What we must do, and can do successfully, is to show the structures of anxiety, of conflicts, of guilt. These structures, which are effective because they mirror what we are, are in us, and if we are right, they are in other people also. If we

bring these structures before them, then it is as if we held up
a mirror in which they see themselves. Whether we shall succeed in this nobody knows. This is the risk we must take. It
is a risk which missionaries have always taken. It cannot be
replaced by evidence. We cannot use evidence to tell people
that human nature is like this. We can do it only in terms of
risk. And this should make us very humble; we can know
what we are (although this is the hardest knowledge of all),
but we do not know what we can become. And we should
not simply measure what we can become by what we are
today.

Then the question arises, which gospel shall we communicate? There is one consolation. None of us is asked to
speak to everybody in all places and in all periods. Communication is a matter of participation. Where there is no participation there is no communication. This is, again, a limiting
condition because our participation is inevitably limited. A
missionary in China for thirty years once said, "Now after
thirty years I have just begun to learn the elements of Chinese
culture and thinking." Yet he was one of the greatest scholars
in Chinese culture. The really serious problem for us is participation. This was much easier for the early Church because
every man in the early Church belonged to the Hellenistic
world which was united under the Roman Empire, where
Jews and Greeks had been mingling long before Christianity.
Paul is the outstanding example.

But this is not our situation today. Communication to
primitive peoples in all missionary fields is always easier than
to more developed and educated people. The reason is that the
character of primitive peoples is less shaped. The difficulty
with the highly developed religions of Asia, for instance, is
not so much that they reject the Christian answer *as answer*,
as that their human nature is formed in such a way that they

do not ask the questions to which the Gospel gives the answer. To them the Christian answer is no answer because they have not asked the question to which Christianity is supposed to give the answer. This is one example of the problem of participation.

There are other illustrations of the problem of participation. In the year 1880 in continental Europe there was an unconditional non-participation in the European churches by the proletariat! The churches were empty. The biggest churches in proletarian sections had no "workers" in them at all, and the ministers thundered against the atheistic masses. But these masses didn't hear them, for they never came to hear them. There was no participation whatever.

Then there was the other side, the European intelligentsia. For them, at least some attempts were made through the theological work in the universities. Yet for the largest part there was non-participation. And measured by the standards of the high cultural development of the European intelligentsia of fifty years ago, the churches seemed to be for these people petty bourgeois barbarism.

We do not need to go into the problem of participation in respect to other groups. We in America know about that! We know about the bitter feeling and the resentment of some of the groups among us, not because of lack of good will but because of our inability to participate. Think of groups like the Jews, the colored peoples, even sometimes the Roman Catholics. Participation means participation in *their* existence, out of which the questions come to which we are supposed to give the answer.

Let us here make an application to our children. With children we have a similar situation. There are two principles we should follow in the religious education of our children. The first is that the questions which are really in the hearts of the children should be answered and the children should be shown that biblical symbols and the Christian message are an answer to just these questions. And secondly, we ought to seek to shape their existence in the direction of the questions which we believe are the more universal ones. This would be similar to what we do with primitive peoples in the mission field. We seek to answer *their* questions and in doing so we, at the same time, slowly transform their existence so that they come to ask the questions to which the Christian message gives the answer.

But sometimes there is not a *lack* of participation but *too much* of it. And that is something which is equally serious and difficult for the situation of ministers. Ministers are a social class, in a special place, in a special period. They are not the well-off middle class, yet they are not so badly off either. They live in a Protestant country which has experienced a Puritan-evangelistic history and later became an industrial society. Ours is a society which tries with all its means, unconsciously and sometimes even consciously, to standardize everything by means of public communication which every moment fills the very air we breathe. So here participation is very easy! In fact, it is so easy that in order to communicate the Gospel we need non-participation. Ministers need withdrawal and retirement from these influences beating upon them every minute. This, perhaps, is the most difficult task. Ministers belong to those who participate, and have only weak weapons to resist this participation.

II.

The foregoing part of the discussion has shown some of the limits of communication. But now we can strike a more positive note. Something has happened in our time, which has opened up many people in such a way that we can again speak to them and can participate in their situation. Today there are many people who have become aware of their human existence in such a way that they ask the question to which we can give the answer. In following this method, we follow the lead of the Beatitudes. There Jesus always points to the situation in which people are and in which they ask for the Kingdom of God. It is then that they can understand the answer, and hence are blest. This method should be followed more consciously by all of us, for it recognizes in the Beatitudes, as in our time, the situation of existential conflict—the conflicts in the very depths of our human existence of longings, of anxiety, and of threatening despair. Since the middle of the nineteenth century, a movement has arisen in the Western world which expresses the anxiety about the meaning of our existence, including the problems of death, faith, and guilt. In our present-day literature many names are given to this phenomenon. Someone has called it "Wasteland," and others speak of "No Exit," or "The Age of Anxiety." Another speaks of the "Neurotic Character of Our Times," and another of "Man Against Himself," and still another about "Encounter with Nothingness."

We can speak to people only if we participate in their concern, not by condescension, but by sharing in it. We can point to the Christian answer only if, on the other hand, we are not identical with them. And thirdly, we can use these people and their ideas to awaken those among our group who are still living in a secure tower. We can awaken them to the elements in themselves which are usually covered by an assumed knowledge of all answers. So these three phases we must keep in mind. We must participate but we must not be identical, and we must use this double attitude to undercut the complacency of those who assume that they know all answers and are not aware of their existential conflicts.

Our answers must have as many forms as there are questions, and situations, individual and social. But there is one thing perhaps which will be common to all our answers if we answer in terms of the Christian message. The Christian message is the message of a new Reality in which we can participate and which gives us the power to take anxiety and despair upon ourselves. *And this we must, and this we can communicate.*

III.

But now we ask, is this the Christian message if we measure it by the Bible and by history? Against this question we ask another: Who can measure it? There is no pope in Protestantism, and if the Bible speaks, it speaks *to us.* Not only is there no pope, there is no council of bishops, no presbyters, no voting of church members on these matters. This was always so. In former centuries of Christian history, the authorities formulated as the biblical message, often unconsciously, those points which gave answers to the temporal and spatial situation of their people, including themselves. They formulated as the biblical message that which could be communicated to themselves as well as to the masses.

In the early Greek church it was the anxiety about death and doubt which prompted the double idea which we find in all the early Greek fathers, namely, that "Life" and "Light" is the message of Christianity. In the Greek Orthodox Church this is still decisive today. Easter is by far the most important festival of the Russian church. In the medieval church, it was the anxiety resulting from the social and spiritual chaos following the breakup of the Roman Empire which produced the transcendent-sacramental foundation of a hierarchical system to guide society and individuals. In the Reformation it was the anxiety of guilt and the message of justification which was decisive for every formula of all the Reformers. In modern Protestantism it has been the message of a religious cultural unity in view of a more personalistic—and in America, more social—conception of the Kingdom of God as a religious cultural unity. If you want to make it schematical, you may say, it was John who influenced the first part of church history; it was Peter who influenced the medieval period; it was Paul who provided the basis for the Reformation; and it was the Jesus of the Synoptics that was the dominant influence for our modern time.

Now we turn again to Paul, but not in the way that the Reformation did. The message which is to be heard by those people of whom we have been speaking is the message of the New Creature—the message of the New Being. Lest we draw a mistaken conclusion here, we must hasten to add that those different messages do not contradict each other. When we speak of the New Being, it includes reconciliation which means what the reformers called "justification by faith" and "forgiveness of sins." It includes the truths for which the early church was searching. It includes participation in the eternal. It includes the Kingdom of God established and fighting in history and related to all cultural content. But the focus in this formulation is different. It centers around what we might call "healing reality," around the courage to say "yes" in the encounter with nothingness, anxiety, and despair.

IV.

Now, what are the consequences of this line of thought in terms of a few important doctrines? First, the doctrine of sin. In the whole period since the beginning of the eighteenth century this has been the most attacked of all doctrines. A term like "original sin" was considered as a shame and as ridiculous. The change today in this regard is tremendous. Perhaps we should not use these words very often because of their traditionalistic and moralistic connotations, and because of the corresponding protest against them. Yet we can describe today in every sermon and address all phases of that aspect of the human situation which Christianity has called "sin." We can describe concupiscence, will-to-power, and *hubris*—the self-elevation of man and such negative consequences of it as self-hate, hostility, self-seclusion, pride, and despair. Today the meaning of original sin, its universality, its tragic role in history, can be emphasized in a way that it could not be twenty years ago. For we are able today to use a concept which everybody understands, the concept of estrangement: estrangement from oneself, from the other man, from the ground out of which we come and to which we go. A profound insight has been developed in modern literature namely, that one of the fundamental expressions of sin is to make the other person into an object, into a thing. This is perhaps the greatest temptation in an industrial society in which everybody is brought into the process of mechanical production and consumption, and even the spiritual life in all its forms is commercialized and subjected to the same process. This happens in every encounter between man and man.

The second point which has been opened up by our situation, and which is a consequence of a concept like the New Being, is the relationship of religion and medicine. This relationship was absolutely clear in the period in which a word like salvation was used for the whole of Christianity. Salvation is healing. This we have rediscovered: a new approach to the meaning of salvation—the original approach. Christianity is not a set of prohibitions and commands. And salvation is not making man better and better. Christianity is the message of a New Reality which makes the fulfillment of our essential being possible. Such being transcends all special prohibitions and commands by one law which is not law, namely love.

Medicine has helped us to rediscover the meaning of grace in our theology. This is perhaps its most important contribution. You cannot help people who are in psychosomatic distress by telling them what to do. You can help them only by giving them something—by accepting them. This means help through the grace which is active in the healing relationship whether it is done by the minister or by the doctor. This, of course, includes the reformation point of view, a view which has also been rediscovered by medicine, namely, you must feel that you have been accepted. Only then can one accept himself. It is never the other way around. That was the plight of Luther in his struggle against the distorted late Roman Church which wanted "that men make themselves first acceptable and then God would accept them." But it is always the other way around. First you must be accepted. Then you can accept yourself, and that means, you can be healed. Illness, in the largest sense of body, soul, and spirit, is estrangement.

A third point has to do with Christology. If we speak of the manifestation of the New Being in Christ, then we do not have to go into matters which involved the early church following its Greek philosophical need. Rightly for that period, but wrongly for us, there was need of a kind of divine-human-nature chemistry. What is understandable for people of our time, and what we can say today, is that we have a message of something which breaks the existential conflict and overcomes estrangement. There is a power from beyond existence which for us is verifiable by participation. This gives quite a different type of Christology. Christ is the place where the New Reality is completely manifest because in him in every moment, the anxiety of finitude and the existential conflicts are overcome. That is his divinity. This means that he is not another law. If he were another law with commandments and prohibitions, he would be just old being and not New Being; he would be just that from which we would need another healer. But he can be the healer because he is not law. Nor do we need for this Christology the sacrifice of the intellect. This again would be a human work. It would be old being, and we would need someone who could liberate us from this old being. What he is, is healing power overcoming estrangement because he himself was not estranged.

Finally, a few words about the Church in the light of the idea of the New Being. The Church is the Community of the New Being. Again and again, people say, "I do not like organized religion." The Church is not organized religion. It is not hierarchical authority. It is not a social organization. It is all of this, of course, but it is primarily a group of people who express a new reality by which they have been grasped. Only *this* is what the Church really means. It is the place where the power of the New Reality which is Christ, and which was prepared in all history and especially in Old Testament history, moves into us and is continued by us.

It can be said, for instance, that the Church is the place where an act of love overcomes the demonic force of objectification—of making people into objects, into things. It is not a new law for social action, but it is the place where we can do a double thing: withdraw from the situation, and attack the situation. The Church is the place where the New Being is real, and the place where we can go to introduce the New Being into reality. It is the continuation of the New Being, even if its organization seems always a betrayal of the New Being. And the New Being which is behind all this is the Divine Being. But the Divine Being is not a being beside others. *It is the power of being conquering non-being.* It is eternity conquering temporality. It is grace conquering sin. It is ultimate reality conquering doubt. From the point of view of the New Being it is the ground of being, and therefore the creator of the New Being. And out of this ground we can get the courage to affirm being, even in a state of doubt, even in anxiety and despair. The New Being includes a new approach to God which is possible even to those who are under the despair of doubt and don't know the way out.

Now a word about the term "stumbling block." Christian ministers often, when they feel frustrated, say that Christianity must be a stumbling block for most people. Nevertheless there are always a few who come to our churches for whom it is not a stumbling block. This gives the minister consolation. But there are two kinds of "stumbling blocks." One is genuine, the one implied in what was said at the beginning of this chapter about genuine decision. There is always a genuine decision against the Gospel for those for whom it is a stumbling block. But this decision should not be dependent on the wrong stumbling block, namely, the wrong way of our communication of the Gospel—our inability to communicate. What we have to do is to overcome the wrong stumbling block in order to bring people face to face with the right stumbling block and enable them to make a genuine decision. Will the Christian churches be able to remove the wrong stumbling blocks in their attempts to communicate the Gospel?

CPSIA information can be obtained at www.ICGtesting.com
Printed in the USA
BVOW08s1215070816

458132BV00001B/2/P